THE GENERATION THAT KNEW NOT JOSEF★

LLOYD BILLINGSLEY

THE GENERATION THAT KNEW NOT JOSEF. ★

A Critique of Marxism and the Religious Left

MULTNOMAH PRESS
PORTLAND, OREGON 97266

By the same author:
   Plays:
      Green Card
      Royal Suite
   Screenplays:
      Multiple Choice
      Best Supporting Role
   Novel:
      A Year For Life

Edited by Rodney L. Morris
Cover design by Larry Ulmer

THE GENERATION THAT KNEW NOT JOSEF
© 1985 by Lloyd Billingsley
Published by Multnomah Press
Portland, Oregon 97266

Printed in the United States of America

Library of Congress Cataloging in Publication Data

Billingsley, Lloyd.
   The generation that knew not Josef.

   Bibliography: p. 211
   Includes index.
   1. Communism and religion.   I. Title.
HX536.B468   1985   335.43   84-27362
ISBN 0-88070-081-5

85 86 87 88 89 90 91 – 10 9 8 7 6 5 4 3 2 1

For all rootless cosmopolitans,
undesirable elements, and
other such strangers and pilgrims
in the earth.

CONTENTS

FOREWORD

Christians have long insisted that theirs is a religion bound up in history. The incarnation, death, and resurrection of Christ are events that happened in space and time, not in some spiritual twilight zone. Yet most American Christians today betray their commitment to a historical religion by perpetuating an astonishing ignorance of the past.

Not long ago, I heard of a young lady whose friends made a passing remark about a recent Reformation Day service at their church. Although she was the product of twelve years of education in a Christian school, she had not heard of nor could she deduce what Reformation Day was. When it was explained to her that the service commemorated the founding of the Protestant Reformation, she casually remarked that her family wasn't Protestant; they were Baptists.

Aside from the possible ecclesiastical ramifications of such a remark, it illustrates a woeful ignorance of history. Not realizing one is a Protestant may be a rather innocuous side effect of being oblivious to the events of earlier ages. More troubling consequences are not only possible, they are often likely, sometimes inevitable.

It is no accident that among Jews, the almost ritualistic refrain regarding the Holocaust is "Never again." Jews understand that memories are fickle and optimistic. It would be easy to forget the obscene and bizarre events that led so many to death, so many more to intense suffering. It would be easy to allow such a painful epoch to degenerate into legend. But in the defiant cry, "Never again," the historicity of the Holocaust is asserted at the same time that the future of Jewish lives is pledged.

Perhaps this sense of history (as well as the searing memory of this particular sequence of events) accounts for the fact that Jews have been the most watchful critics of what Jean-Francois Revel has called "the totalitarian temptation." Christians have been much less attentive and much less wary of the utopian promises held out by Marxist-Leninist prophets.

This may be because theologically conservative Christians have always been suspicious of thinking too much about politics. In most conservative churches, the only people who paid any attention to international politics were missionaries. And they had a calling to preach; they didn't dare endanger their visas by criticizing the local regime. As long as the "powers that were" in any given country allowed the preaching of the gospel, little attention was paid to political philosophies or their effects.

While American evangelicals have tacitly endorsed democracy and eschewed totalitarianism, their political thinking has tended to be pragmatic, considering only the interests of the church's evangelistic needs. They have rarely given much attention to political theory.

So historical ignorance has been compounded by theoretical incompetence, all made worse by the lack of familiarity with the intellectual eddies of the past five decades. How many Christians who loudly pronounce on matters political are aware of anything by Orwell other than 1984? How many are familiar with the political sojourn of Arthur Koestler, with the insights into totalitarianism from Hannah Arendt, with the warnings of the "road to serfdom" from Friedrich A. Hayek, with the struggles of Trotskyite Sidney Hook against Stalinism, with the analysis of Marxism from Raymond Aron or Michael Polanyi, with the role of Reinhold Niebuhr in the formation of post-war liberalism?

Or more recently, how many have contended with the reflections of philosopher William Barrett on the "truancy" of American intellectuals in the 1930s and 1940s? How many have studied the accounts of enthusiasts for the "new socialist man" in Paul Hollander's study, *Political Pilgrims?* How many know what Susan Sontag said in her Town Hall speech in 1981? How many have wrestled with the challenges presented by Paul Johnson's account of *Modern Times?*

All these writers and thinkers have lessons from history to teach us. They are lessons about our recent history and about our possible futures, lessons that must be learned if we are to behave responsibly as Christians concerned about political issues. Serious statements about politics, including suggestions for particular policies, require some understanding of history. Programs which ignorantly suggest the repetition of past failures must be recognized as the folly of those who are truants from reality.

Rather than apply themselves to the lessons of history, evangelicals with conservative political sentiments have been busy building media empires and mastering direct mail techniques, while those who consider themselves radical have been intoning verses from Amos with mantra-like predictability. Those who take pride in being moderate often mean that they have no firm political convictions at all, and divide their time between fundy-bashing and eagerly securing the acceptance of "progressive" people, that inner ring of New Class intellectuals whose secret hopes usually include the withering away of religion.

It is a dismal scene indeed. Lloyd Billingsley's book offers some welcome refreshment. It will not change the world. But it may prove to some that attention to history is always rewarded. It comes at a time when the nostrums of the left are being challenged around the world, not least significantly within the American Democratic party. One hopes that this book will encourage a new realism that may prevail among American Christians, who have a unique opportunity to care for men and women in this world as they eagerly await the next.

Kenneth A. Myers
Executive Editor
Eternity

ACKNOWLEDGMENTS

Acknowledgment is gratefully made to the following for permission to reprint previously published material:

Catholicism in Crisis: Excerpt from "Why the Church Is Not Pacifist," by Michael Novak. Used by permission.

Editions Stanké: Excerpts from *Mes Dix Annees D'exil a Cuba* by Pierre Charette, © 1979 by Alain Stanké. Used by permission. Special thanks to Marie-Jeanne Dupis for the English translation.

Harcourt Brace Jovanovich, Inc.: Excerpts from *The Origins of Totalitarianism*, © 1951 by Hannah Arendt, renewed 1979 by Mary McCarthy West; excerpts from *The New Class* by Milovan Djilas, © 1957 by Harcourt Brace Jovanovich, Inc.; excerpts from *Memoir of a Revolutionary* by Milovan Djilas, © 1973 by Harcourt Brace Jovanovich, Inc.; excerpts from *Conversations with Stalin* by Milovan Djilas, © 1962 by Harcourt Brace Jovanovich, Inc.; excerpt from "The Prevention of Literature" in *Shooting an Elephant and other Essays* by George Orwell, © 1950 by Sonia Brownell Orwell, renewed 1978 by Sonia Pitt-Rivers; excerpts from "A Reply to Professor Haldane" in *Of Other Worlds* by C. S. Lewis, © 1966 by The Executors of the Estate of C. S. Lewis. Reprinted by permission of Harcourt Brace Jovanovich, Inc.

Excerpt from "Politics and the English Language," © 1946 by Sonia Brownell Orwell, renewed 1974 by Sonia Orwell, excerpted and reprinted in *Shooting an Elephant and Other Essays* by George Orwell. Reprinted by permission of Harcourt Brace Jovanovich, Inc., the estate of the late Sonia Brownell Orwell, and Martin Secker & Warburg Ltd.

Harper and Row Publishers: Quotations of Arthur Koestler from *The God That Failed* by Richard Crossman, Editor, © 1949 by Richard Crossman. Reprinted by permission of Harper & Row, Publishers, Inc. and A. D. Peters & Company Ltd. Acknowledgment is also made to Regnery Gateway, Inc.

Quotations of André Gide, translated and edited by Enid Starkie, from *The God That Failed* by Richard Crossman, Editor, © 1949 by Richard Crossman. Reprinted by permission of Harper & Row,

14 **ACKNOWLEDGMENTS**

Publishers, Inc. and Hamish Hamilton Limited. Acknowledgment is also made to Regnery Gateway, Inc.

Quotations by Soviet official M. Y. Latsis from *Modern Times: The World from the Twenties to the Eighties* by Paul Johnson, © 1983 by Paul Johnson. Reprinted by permission of Harper & Row, Publishers, Inc. and George Weidenfeld & Nicolson Ltd.

Macleans's Magazine: Excerpt from "Some Writers Are More Equal than Others," © 1981 by Barbara Amiel. Used by permission of the author.

Macmillan Publishing Company: Excerpts from *Arrow in the Blue* by Arthur Koestler, © 1952, and renewed 1980, by Arthur Koestler; excerpts from *The Invisible Writing* by Arthur Koestler, © 1954, and renewed 1982, by Arthur Koestler. Used by permission of Macmillan Publishing Company.

The Miami Herald: Excerpts from "Nicaraguan Decries Need for Vote" by Juan Tamayo. Reprinted with permission of the *Miami Herald.*

William Morrow and Company, Inc. and David Higham Associates Limited: Excerpts from *Like It Was: The Diaries of Malcolm Muggeridge,* © 1981 by Malcolm Muggeridge; excerpts from *Things Past* by Malcolm Muggeridge, edited by Ian A. Hunter, © 1934 by Malcolm Muggeridge; excerpts from *Chronicles of Wasted Time,* vol. 1: *The Green Stick* by Malcolm Muggeridge, © 1972 by Malcolm Muggeridge. Used by permission of William Morrow & Company and by permission of David Higham Associates Limited. Acknowledgment is also made to Collins Publishers.

The New York Times: Excerpt from the article by John Vinocur, © 1984 by The New York Times Company. Reprinted by permission.

Martin Secker and Warburg Limited: Excerpts from *George Orwell: A Life* by Bernard Crick, © 1980 by Bernard Crick. Used by permission. Acknowledgment is also made to Little, Brown and Company.

Certainly it is true that the stairway of history is forever echoing with the wooden shoe going up, the polished boot descending.
Peter Viereck

Liberty is an acknowledgement of faith in God and his works.
Frederic Bastiat

INTRODUCTION

> The earnest Freethinkers need not worry themselves so
> much about the persecutions of the past. Before the Liberal
> idea is dead or triumphant, we shall see wars and persecu-
> tions the like of which the world has never seen.
>
> G. K. Chesterton, 1905

The twentieth-century mind, which readily claims superiority to ages past, often displays an extraordinarily short
or selective memory. While flights to the moon, the splitting
of the atom, and the lives of film stars command much attention, other important developments have been passed over
or, more often, willfully ignored.

This is partially understandable. The sages of the past
who pried away at the dilemmas of their time often faced a
paucity of data. Today, the problem is not only the super-
abundance of information, which blurs the edges of truth
like snow, but its fraudulence. "In the end was the lie, and
the lie dwelt among us, graceless and false," would be a true
twentieth-century text. George Orwell doubted whether an
accurate history of modern times could even be written.[1]

This century has also been quite exceptionally destruc-
tive and murderous while claiming the contrary. Many of
those who most dealt in the fool's-gold words of progress—"a
new age" and so on—have been in reality the greatest tyrants
of all time: Hitler, Mussolini, Mao Tse-tung. But Josef Stalin
stands head and shoulders above the rest.

What has been surprisingly, or perhaps not surprisingly, overlooked is that the very luminaries of the Western world, allegedly its brightest, wisest, most creative and compassionate people—the Huxleys, George Bernard Shaw, Jean-Paul Sartre, Eleanor Roosevelt, Pablo Neruda, Dean Hewlett Johnson of Canterbury, and countless others—practiced what André Gide called "Stalinatry." In the rise of Stalin and the Soviet regime, they had seen the Future, and it worked. Stalin, in their view, was for the most part considered as wise as Confucius, as compassionate as Buddha, as efficient as Marcus Aurelius, as popular as Rudolph Valentino. The Reverend Johnson, shedding new light on prophetic interpretation, even suggested that Stalin was ushering in the very kingdom of Christ on earth.

Facing a spectacle of such proportions, one gropes for comparisons. It was as if Ovid, Plato, Galileo, Sophocles, and a few of the church fathers had collaborated on a flowery panegyric for Alaric of the Visigoths. Or in a modern setting, if the Greenpeace organization issued a plea for the immediate slaughter of all baby seals with nuclear weapons.

The discovery of this, to me, stupendous fact that the intellectual samurai of a generation had worshiped quite possibly the greatest mass murderer in history played a large role in shaping my own thinking. If Sartre, Huxley et al were so wrong about something so basic, why listen to them on anything else?

Yet when the matter comes up in discussion, it is immediately apparent that the record is not widely known. It began to occur to me that some benefit might be attained by a work of, as it were, intellectual archeology. As in ancient Egypt, a new generation has arisen, and it knows neither Josef nor his followers nor, one should add, his ex-followers.

Of course, there were exceptions (Bertrand Russell and H. G. Wells, to their great credit, among them) but the trend in the thirties and forties was essentially one of capitulation to totalitarianism. Those who resisted the zeitgeist were often ridiculed, called liars, and had difficulty publishing their writings. Orwell's *Animal Farm*, one of the few works of genius this century has produced, was rejected by *fourteen* publishers as being too hostile to the Soviet regime. One of the rejectors was T. S. Eliot on behalf of Faber and Faber.[2] The tide of Orwelliana in 1984 not only failed to uncover this fact but, for the most part, has been woefully wide of the mark. For instance, media icon Walter Cronkite discussed *1984* without once mentioning communism, about which Orwell had more than a few things to say. It was like discussing the Bible without mentioning Christianity.

Where some people erred was to go and live in the USSR. A few of these left the regime totally disillusioned and strongly anti-utopian. Ignoring the experiences of this small band would be like a scholar of lunar interests refusing to ask Neil Armstrong, "What was it like on the moon?" Yet, many firsthand reports have been scorned.

This too is understandable. These anti-utopians are, after all, fallen angels who have the shockingly bad taste to reveal that Heaven on Earth is not all it is cracked up to be. Some of them even display the outrageous gall to prefer Pie in the Sky of Christian recipe to any sort of pie on the earth, particularly the socialist variety. This group needs to be brought into the present debate.

That debate concerns the new utopias, the Third World Marxist regimes. Do these represent something new, as we are often told? Or are they old Stalin-ware just shined up a bit?

Likewise, are the Western supporters of these regimes, particularly in the church, a new breed? Or are they simply carrying on a well-established apologetic tradition?

Do we welcome those who come in the name of Science and Liberation as allies of the church? Or should our response be that of the man in Jesus' parable: "An enemy has done this."[3]

Is the dialogue between Marxism and Christianity— two religions whose basic tenets are opposed—to be taken seriously? Or is it a joke of cosmic dimensions?

Furthermore, have those who, in the name of Christ, are most critical of the basic institutions of the West ever been brought under the same scrutiny to which they subject everyone else?

The answers to these questions take us into politics. But, as Orwell contended, there is no such thing as staying out of politics. Writing this book, I experienced no threats from any secret police. Neither am I under any obligation to submit my work to censors. Works I might wish to consult, such as *Animal Farm* or *The Gulag Archipelago* are readily available. But if my house lay within the jurisdiction of, say, General Jaruzelski or Fidel Castro this would not be the case. Russian writer Vladimir Voinovich (now exiled), when asked how he wrote his novels, explained, "I write a chapter and hide it. Then, I write another chapter and hide that one too."

Personal freedom, in its traditional sense, is a decidedly unpopular concept today, particularly among Christians. All this may be a matter of indifference to others, but I cannot pretend that it is of no importance to me. Neither, ultimately, can any of us.

INTRODUCTION, NOTES
1. George Orwell, "The Prevention of Literature," in *Inside the Whale and Other Essays* (London: Penguin Books, 1957), 163.
2. Bernard Crick, *George Orwell, A Life* (London: Secker and Warburg, 1980), 315.
3. Matthew 13:28.

PART

1

THE GENERATION
THAT KNEW JOSEF

*Thus Liberalism had become a habit with Oblonsky and he enjoyed his news-
paper, as he did his after-dinner cigar, for the slight haze it produced in his brain.*
                                                    Tolstoy, *Anna Karenina*

SECTION 1
ADULATION

CHAPTER 1
TOTALITARIANISM

In a country where the sole employer is the state, opposition
means death by slow starvation. The old principle: who does
not work shall not eat, has been replaced by a new one: who
does not obey shall not eat.   Trotsky, 1937

By the 1980s, so the prophecies went a century ago,
the world would become a heavenly commune. By trampling
down the ignorance and superstition of the past and
cooperating with his fellow beings out of the goodness and
inherent unselfishness of his heart, mankind would achieve
the elimination of sin, the conquest of disease, the perfec-
tion of genius, and the invention of immortality. Wars and
tumults would follow the brontosaurus into extinction;
peace would rule the globe. World's fairs around the turn of
the century displayed scenarios that envisioned us all living
in domed, climate-controlled cities; safe, sanitized, and per-
fected forever, our whims catered to by robots; all needs met,
all anxieties tranquilized, free hors d'oeuvres in every restau-
rant and bar.

Just how this global Manifest Destiny would be
achieved, let alone sustained, was not explained but rather
accepted as an article of Progressive Faith. Somehow, Mankind, following the yellow brick road of Science, would ar-
rive at the collective Oz.

What actually happened turned out quite different.
The majority of people in the world today live in conditions

as subutopian as possible, sometimes under murderous dictators of all ideologies, from Enver Hoxha's Albania to the Ayatollah Khomeini's Iran. Those who think this sort of statement simplistic might try, in good democratic style, to count those countries with a healthy degree of freedom from tyranny. There are about thirty in a world where nations number well into the hundreds.

Totalitarianism, the absolute power of rulers over their subjects, exists. It is the dominant force in dozens of countries, including the largest and most militarily powerful in history—the USSR. A complete study of the rise of totalitarianism is beyond the scope of this book. Hannah Arendt's *Origins of Totalitarianism* and Paul Johnson's *Modern Times* best tell the story. And it is a sad story indeed.

In the past sixty years there has been more brutality and obscurantism, more senseless conflicts, more of the past's heritage destroyed, more crass idolatry, more lies and hoaxes perpetrated, more people murdered or cast adrift as undesirable elements than in any other time in history; most of this in purportedly just causes for the advancement of mankind in general. The individual has not fared well.

Why has all this happened? What has gone wrong? Where is the promise of the nineteenth century?

Exiled Russian writer Aleksandr Solzhenitsyn has said, "Man has forgotten God, that is why all this has happened." Hearing this sort of analysis, trendy Westerners groan, look up from the latest copy of *Time* magazine (where they read that Yuri Andropov was a closet liberal, kind of a Soviet Bill Moyers) point to their Ph.D.s from Columbia or the London School of Economics, shake their heads, and aim their barbs of "simplistic" at the author of *The Gulag Archipelago*. But Solzhenitsyn is not the first to have diagnosed the situation in what might be called spiritual terms.

Arthur Koestler casually remarked in his autobiography *Arrow In The Blue* that the place of God has been vacant in the West since the end of the eighteenth century. This was a curious statement for someone who his entire life disdained all traditional religion. In his case, turning his back on God meant seeking heaven in the new, earthly utopias. The same thing has happened on a larger scale with humanity in general. As Chesterton observed, when people cease to believe in God they do not wind up believing in nothing but, what is worse, in anything, however bogus. Since the Enlightenment there has been, as Koestler observed, a vacuum in the West. Recent history is, for the most part, how that vacuum has been filled. Evil men—no other word will do—have not been reluctant to step into the void.

This does not mean that the twentieth century has not been a religious age, for that is precisely the case. Man continues to be *homo religioso,* ever zealous in the service of new secular divinities whether in the capacity of clergy or laity.

What this represented practically and politically for a sizeable chunk of the world was a return to Theocracy; the new deities being 'History' or 'The Race' and their vicars and inquisitors, the various gangster-statesmen such as Lenin, Mao, Mussolini, Hitler, and Stalin. C.S. Lewis, who was reluctant to write on political themes, nevertheless found it necessary to touch on the subject while defending himself from attacks by British scientist and left-wing polemicist J. B. S. Haldane.

> I am a democrat because I believe that no man or group of men is good enough to be trusted with uncontrolled power over others. And the higher the pretensions of such power, the more dangerous I think it both to the rulers and to the subjects. Hence Theocracy is the worst of all governments. If we must have a tyrant a robber baron is far better than an inquisitor. The baron's cruelty may sometimes sleep, his cupidity at some point be sated; and since he dimly knows he is going wrong he may possibly repent. But the inquisitor who mistakes his own cruelty and lust of power and fear for the voice of Heaven will torment us infinitely because he torments us with the approval of his own conscience and his better impulses appear to him as temptations.[1]

With national socialism having died with Hitler in his bunker and with fascism left hanging upside down with

Mussolini, Marxism-Leninism remains the major Theocracy of our time. In fact, Marxism-Leninism is best described as successful fascism. Mussolini and Hitler, after all, were both socialists, 'Nazi' being an abbreviation for 'national socialist'. (The term is proscribed in the USSR and 'Hitlerism' used in its place.) I use 'socialism' and 'communism' interchangeabley, since the Union of Soviet *Socialist* Republics also does so. The desired end product is the same: a society "scientifically" controlled and planned by a bureaucratic elite whether achieved, as in the elusive schemes of "democratic" socialists, by evolution and ballots or, as on the more militant, fundamentalist side of the Theocracy, with revolution and bullets. It can be put no better than by French writer Bernard-Henri Lévy—socialism is the god of this age.

With the place of God vacant in so many people and their hopes for an afterlife thus destroyed, their attention is necessarily focused on the here and now. Hence there have been and continue to be multitudes who gladly exchange freedom for security, and who show remarkable credulity in accepting the promises of any demagogue who promises such phantom concepts as 'a new and happy life.' Without people willing to make the freedom-for-security exchange, the whole system breaks down.

People who made the trade do not necessarily get security. What they do get is the dubious privilege of being raw material for this century's most prevalent vice—social engineering. With God out of the way, there is nothing special—like a soul for instance—in man, hence he may be shoveled around like concrete at the whims of "planners" who, being trained in the proper dialectic, know what is best.

These planners must necessarily be seen as infallible when they speak ex cathedra. The language used of them is blatantly religious: Our Wise Leader, the Great Helmsman, and so on. If buildings plastered with pictures five meters square of Mao Tse-tung and myriads of his subjects waving their little red books and chanting the author's praises is not idolatry , then nothing is.

The theological doctrine used to sustain the fiction of a wise, infallible planner is a representational one similar to the New Testament teaching that Jesus Christ is the Head of the church and the representative of all Christians. Socialist rulers are, by their own description, the Dictatorship of the Proletariat. All the aspirations of the people are held to be embodied in the rulers, an abstraction similar to but far transcending French King Louis XIV's, *L'Etat, c'est moi.* Socialist dictators not only represent the people, according to the theory; they *are* the people. The key to Communist party antagonism to the independent Solidarity trade union in Poland is that any labor institution independent of the government explodes the notion that the Socialist government represents the best interest of the workers. Workers, after all, have seldom desired scarcity of goods, low wages, and martial law for themselves. What amazes is that the Soviet Union has not invaded, as they did in Hungary and Czechoslovakia, when vassal states displayed the arrogance of even considering rank heresies like loosening controls on censorship.

The dictatorship of the proletariat in any Marxist Theocracy is not merely implementing a political program. They see themselves not as mere public officials but as the incarnations of the Will of History, carrying out its mandates. History, according to their eschatology, is progressing inexorably toward a perfect socialist state. This is held to be inevitable. How do they know? On what science is this based? Marx and Engels said so, they believe it, and that settles it.

In the end, as Marx explained, the state itself would fade away. It is not exactly clear how long the world would have to wait for this momentous event, but those intrepid souls who study Marx indicate that he expected two generations to do the job. It has not happened. The theocratic states now take more power for themselves, not less.

It is curious today that in conversing with people of high intelligence and education, who are informed about the space shuttle, sociobiology, and the politics of, say, Pakistan, stating a belief in a traditional afterlife causes stares of amazement, as if one had confessed to being arrested for indecent exposure in New York's Central Park. But to adhere to a preposterous and impossible notion such as the withering away of the state when, in fact, socialism is based on a preponderant, omnipotent government, draws no cries of derision. There is no precedent in history for believing that the state will fade away, much less any rational basis for the creed. But then, one notices how small a part reason has played in human affairs in this century. Rather, in dealing with some minds, one must slog through a reeking bog of irrationality, fitting terrain for the growth of totalitarian ideas fertilized with heaping shovels of pseudoscientific manure and watered with the intoxicating chemicals of hysterical rhetoric.

An Eastern bloc athlete (who wisely maintained his anonymity) at a recent track meet in Austria quipped, "If Marx was a scientist, why didn't he first try communism on rats?" The current received wisdom is that Marx was a scientist and that socialism is scientific, as opposed to the allegedly wasteful, anarchic Western democracies where—horror of horrors—people are allowed to do as they please, initiate their own economic activity, and maintain backward superstitions like Judaism and Christianity.

Marx studied classics; his scientific credentials were at best dubious. He followed the scientific charlatan Pierre Trémaux, calling him greater than Darwin, and put much stock in discredited and false concepts like phrenology, which extrapolates character and intelligence from the shape of the skull.[2] Hitler held similar ideas. It is indeed amazing that sociologists often hold Marx in esteem since he considered groups such as Indians backward, barbaric, "non-historical people." That minority civil rights activists revere him is even more remarkable since he regularly used racial epithets like "nigger" and "kike" in his correspondence, often referring to his own relatives. Like Trémaux, he believed that blacks were not evolved apes but degenerated men.[3] Sadly, this dimension of the *enragé* in the reading room of the British Museum has not come to light. Even Christians continue to speak of his insights.[4]

Marx dealt not in testable data but in predictive prophecies that for the most part have not only been unfulfilled, but the exact opposite has happened. To cite one example, capitalism has not collapsed as he predicted. On the contrary, the lot of the Western worker has improved, not worsened. The Leninist explanation of this, parroted so frequently by churchmen, that the exploitation has been transferred to the international scene simply does not stand up. Those Third World countries that have had most contact with the West have achieved higher standards of living than those that have not. To link Western presence with poverty explains nothing and begs the question of why the countries were poor before they had any contact with outsiders.

The empirical data show that socialist theocracies, far from relieving poverty, create it. Socialist states have failed at providing the basic necessities of life and have become importers of food where, in presocialist times, they exported commodities such as grain. Czarist Russia exported wheat; now they buy it from the nefarious, allegedly inefficient West.

Given the premise of the socialist theocracy that history is progressing toward a collectivist utopia, political morality becomes very simple. It is not enough to wait for utopia to come. One must help things along by agitation, organization, propaganda, and all forms of struggle, including violence and betraying one's bourgeois friends and relatives. Whatever advances progress is the supreme moral duty and abrogates all other moral considerations. On this subject C.S. Lewis observed:

> In this state of mind, men can become devil-worshippers
> in the sense that they can now *honor*, as well as obey, their
> own vices. All men at times obey their vices; but it is when
> cruelty, envy, and lust of power appear as the commands of a
> great super-personal force that they can be exercised with
> self-approval. The first symptom is in language. When to
> 'kill' becomes to 'liquidate' the process has begun. The
> pseudo-scientific word disinfects the thing of blood and
> tears, or pity and shame, and mercy itself can be regarded as a
> sort of untidiness.[5]

Hatred is one of the fundamentals of the new theocracies. An American Communist party spokesman addressing a California audience in 1979 appealed for funds by saying, "if there is an ounce of hatred in you, give." Cuban revolutionary hero Ernesto "Che" Guevara declared, "We must develop hatred in order to transform man into a machine for killing."[6] The July 7, 1984 issue of *Pravda* editorialized, "A feeling of love toward the motherland, and a feeling of hatred toward its enemies, must be instilled in young people with ever-increasing persistence. . . ."

Class hatred and conflicts, in the Marxist view, are entirely natural and inevitable. The bourgeoisie, the owning class, battles the proletariat, the working class. The conflict will continue until the Right Side wins. With the spiritual, transcendent dimension eliminated, the carriers of evil are all contemporary. Hence, the ferocity with which they are eliminated.

In Orwell's *Animal Farm*, the pigs, having taken over the farm from Jones, hold a meeting. One item for discussion is the question whether wild, nondomesticated creatures such as rats are comrades. The animals' politburo, headed by the pigs, deliberates and decides that rats indeed are comrades, with the cat voting on both sides. From the pigs' point of view, it was a wise decision. Totalitarianism involves an alliance of the elite and the mob. The violent, criminal element, once in power, can ply their trade with complete safety and even approval. Joseph Conrad made the point in 1911 in his novel *Under Western Eyes:*

> In a real revolution, the best characters do not come to the front. A violent revolution falls into the hands of narrow-minded fanatics and of tyrannical hypocrites at first. Afterwards comes the turn of all the pretentious intellectual failures of the time. Such are the chiefs and leaders. You will notice that I have left out the mere rogues. The scrupulous and the just, the noble, humane and devoted natures, the unselfish and the intelligent may begin a movement but it passes away from them. They are not the leaders of a revolution. They are its victims: the victims of disgust, disenchantment—often of remorse. Hopes grotesquely betrayed, ideals caricatured—that's the definition of revolutionary success.[7]

This is more than theory. Collectivization is impossible without terror. Any socialist leader who does not have the stomach for implementing terror does not last long. Perhaps this was the reason for the murder of Grenadian revolutionary Maurice Bishop. The dictatorship of the proletariat does not believe in the oxymoron, 'democratic socialism.' Under these conditions, as Conrad wrote, the ruthless power-worshipers rise to the top. They make no apology for their tactics, as Soviet secret police official M.Y. Latsis explained during the great purges:

> We are not carrying out war against individuals. We are exterminating the bourgeoisie as a class. We are not looking for evidence of witnesses to reveal the deeds or words against the Soviet power. The first question we ask is—to what class does he belong, what are his origins, upbringing, education or profession? These questions define the fate of the accused. This the essence of the Red terror.[8]

The great need of socialist theocracy is for an effective demonology. As under Hitler, Jews are suspect. In addition to the hatred of the bourgeoisie, anti-Semitism is baptized under the euphemism of combating the influence of "rootless cosmopolitans." Hence, to have traveled, to know foreign languages, to be broadminded is a crime. Given the nature of the Theocracy, this is not surprising. Any ideology that explains all history and even the future cannot tolerate people who are creative, spontaneous, and who advance ideas that nobody, especially the leaders, foresaw.

The class-struggle hatred has also been translated to the international scene. The animosity directed toward, particularly, the United States is, from the theocratic standpoint, understandable. There must be some large, visible entity to blame for their own utter failures. And the theocracies have failed at everything except military conquest and deluding people in the West. Peaceful coexistence with the West is viewed by the dictatorship of the proletariat as only a temporary stage, a rest stop on the highway of progress. The theocratic position is that there can be no real peace until the entire world bourgeoisie has been somehow eliminated as a class. Thus, the class-struggle jihad continues and will continue. It is socialism's Final Solution.

Every word and action of socialist dictators confirms these goals and concepts. They are reaffirmed at every party congress. Still one often hears, in spite of the overwhelming evidence, that the dictatorship of the proletariat has changed; they have mellowed or grown. Far from promoting a violent struggle, we are told, they are actually in the process of settling down to a Scandinavian-style existence which they could achieve if only those awful, strident people in the American government and NATO would stop making them afraid.

To say that militant, nuclear-armed theocracies like the Soviet Union are no longer expansionist is, to me, the most ludicrous position that could be advanced; like saying that Billy Graham has really been traveling around the world all these years promoting sodomy. In my lifetime, the USSR has invaded Hungary and Czechoslovakia. As I write this, there are over one hundred thousand Soviet troops in Afghanistan—one of the poorest Third World countries—busy with tanks and helicopters and executions, initiating the Afghans to true Socialist Realism, bombing them into the next stage of history. The socialist theocracy is indeed evangelistically zealous, more so than any band of Jesuits ever were among the Aztecs. The Marxist gospel is spread with the sword. With communist leaders scarcely concealing their aims (Khrushchev's "We will bury you!"), the burden of proof is on those who say that the dictatorship of the proletariat is *not* expansionist.

All this moral relativism in monstrous incarnation also involves a great deal of disinformation. The organized lying practiced by totalitarian states is not, as is often contended, a temporary expedient like military deception in wartime but rather a permanent feature of totalitarianism. During the aftermath of the downing of Korean Air Lines Flight 007 by a Soviet fighter (the Russian government recently decorated the pilot) in which nearly three hundred innocent, defenseless people were murdered, one could take any official Soviet statement, count the lies, and easily get into double figures. (One sure tip of a coming lie, a big one, is the preface, "as is well known," usually followed by something like "Britain has been planning nuclear war for three years.") The only believable statement came from a Russian general who said, without a trace of embarrassment, "We would do it again."

Modern technology—especially television—is well suited to the spread and maintenance of lies. One shudders to think what Hitler would have done with the medium. But there is more. Electronics makes surveillance easier. Modern weapons help with what may be termed 'crowd control.' Up-to-date techniques of wallbuilding and barbed-wire stringing, complete with sensitive mines and automatically firing guns, make escape from East Germany, a wholly-owned subsidiary of the USSR, a risky business. In addition, entire professional disciplines such as psychiatry, education, and medicine can be harnessed to propaganda that maintains the illusions of infallibility of the dictatorship of the proletariat and also punishes ("reeducates") those who dissent from the party line.

What is the party line? In theory, the dictates of history; in reality, nothing more than the views of a few very old, ambitious, humorless, dogmatic, and not very intelligent men. To deviate from this line is to be branded insane and tossed into mental asylums like the Serbsky Institute, as

Victor Nekipelov has described in his book, *Institute of Fools*. Solzhenitsyn has written how doctors take part in interrogations, informing the inquisitors/torturers when the victim has had enough. Then, they keep him alive for the next shift.

The new theocrats have all the tools. Ivan the Terrible would have been envious. He was content to control all political power but was not totalitarian. His repressive apparatus was always inefficient, the ruling classes half-apathetic or half-liberal. On top on this, the prevailing religious doctrine militated against perfectionism and infallibility. Contemporary autocracies are very much in the same position.

The socialist theocracy, on the other hand, *is* the state religion. It controls everyone and everything within its ever-expanding parish.

That, ultimately, is what totalitarianism is all about—power and control. Marxism, far from a science, is a rationale for the claim of unlimited power. As Lenin put it—who whom?—who gives orders to whom; who has the guns, the power. The new, materialist deities, possessing this power, believe they can do all, as Hannah Arendt explains:

> Until now the totalitarian belief that everything is possible seems to have proved only that everything can be destroyed. Yet, in their effort to prove that everything is possible, totalitarian regimes have discovered without knowing it that there are crimes which men can neither punish nor forgive. When the impossible was made possible it became the unpunishable, unforgivable absolute evil which could no longer be understood and explained by the evil motives of self-interest, greed, covetousness, resentment, lust for power, and cowardice; and which therefore anger could not revenge, love could not endure, friendship could not forgive. Just as the victims in the death factories or the holes of oblivion are no longer "human" in the eyes of their executioners so this newest species of criminals is beyond the pale even of solidarity in human sinfulness.[9]

Spurning God, man becomes subject to the power and torments of genocidal dictators; trading freedom for security he gets neither, only a new slavery; rejecting absolute standards, he is victimized by absolute evil. Looking for happiness through the senses and a utopia brought in by power, he finds himself trapped in the various bastions of materialist puritanism, the dreariest and shabbiest regimes ever to exist on earth.

Many tyrannies—feudalism for example—have come and gone. Others, like national socialism (Nazism) have been fought and vanquished. Where Generalissimo Franco ruled for decades, there now sits an elected Spanish government. But there exist no instances of liberation from an entrenched socialist theocracy. As Lenin said, "If we go, we shall slam the door on an empty house."

The story of our time reads like a tragic novel. Observing the situation from a free state where one may go where one wishes, believe what one chooses, and write what one pleases, and where opportunities and the material needs of life are abundantly available, one feels like Ralph, a boy in William Golding's novel *Lord of the Flies*. Safe in the hands of rescuers, he remembered the earlier, happier days on the island before idolatry, hatred, and violence turned it into a black, smoking ruin. Thinking of everything that had happened, Ralph felt a great sorrow wrench his entire being. Tears poured down his face as he wept for the end of innocence, for his murdered friend, and for the darkness of man's heart.

CHAPTER 1, NOTES
1. C.S. Lewis, "A Reply to Professor Haldane," in *Of Other Worlds* (New York: Harcourt, Brace, World, 1967), 81.
2. Nathaniel Weyl, *Karl Marx, Racist* (New York: Arlington, 1979), 22.
3. Ibid., 131-36.
4. David Lyon, "If Marx Is dead, What Is All the Fuss About?", *His*, April 1984, 19.
5. Lewis, *Of Other Worlds*, 84.
6. Jacques Ellul, *Violence* (New York: Seabury, 1969), 104.
7. Joseph Conrad, *Under Western Eyes* (New York: New Directions, 1951), 134-35.
8. M.Y. Latsis, quoted in Paul Johnson, *Modern Times* (New York: Harper and Row, 1983), 71.
9. Hannah Arendt, *Origins of Totalitarianism* (New York: Harcourt Brace Jovanovich, 1966), 459.

CHAPTER 2
STALIN

Lest anyone should consider any of this discussion of totalitarianism as existing solely in the realm of theory, it is necessary to examine specific examples. The mass murder of some six million Jews under Hitler is well documented in numerous books, dramatic films, and documentaries. One can to this day visit the very places, such as Auschwitz, where victims were incinerated. In spite of all the evidence, including confessions of those who worked in the death camps, there are those who perversely deny that any holocaust even took place.

Likewise there are those who deny that genocide occurred under Stalin. All the more reason to focus attention on him, for Stalin is the incarnation of totalitarianism.

A large percentage of the generation that knew Joseph Stalin died as a direct result of his directives. These were purely political killings, "exterminations," "liquidations" of "the enemy class" and "undesirable elements." How many were involved? Solzhenitsyn's estimates reach as high as sixty million. Robert Conquest, author of *The Great Terror*, fixed the number at well into the millions.[1] It is doubtful if we will ever know the true total—God alone knows.

Hitler carried out genocide against those he had

declared his enemies—principally the Jews. Stalin shared no such high scruples; he attacked at random his own subjects and supporters. And since he had a much longer period of time to operate in and a greater pool of victims from which to choose, there are sound reasons for believing that he killed far more than Hitler.

Collectivization is impossible without terror, and many of the victims were simply slaughtered in the implementation of the first agricultural Five-Year Plan. Entire villages were wiped out. Anyone who in any way resisted the collectivization plan was either killed or shipped off to a labor camp. The victims, of course, were defenseless. There was no armed counterrevolution at the time; Stalin was his own counterrevolution. No one was safe. The purges of the late thirties eliminated many of the early Bolsheviks—after show trials so fraudulent that only a credulous fool (as will be seen, a species in plentiful supply) could have accepted them as genuine. Stalin likewise eliminated many of his top generals and military strategists—an act that played a large role in early Soviet defeats at the hands of the Germans.

Accounts of the terror, such as *The Gulag Archipelago*, *The Great Terror*, and *Kolyma: The Arctic Death Camps*, do not make for pleasant reading. For the millions of victims, there was the visit—always at night—of the secret police, a hard ring of faces around a bed, an arrest, and a quick ride to prison.

After the usual beatings, tortures, interrogations, and forced confessions, the victim was kangaroo-courted into the gulag, which meant a long train ride in conditions barely suitable for livestock. If the destination was Kolyma, there was also a sea voyage from Vladivostok to Magadan. On this passage, guards doused unruly prisoners with frigid sea water pumped through fire hoses.

In the various camps, millions of men and women were literally worked to death. Prisoners from the warmer climates often died on their first day in the arctic cold. Religious believers were tossed in with hardened criminals.

Guards often shot people simply for their own amusement. Anything that would have smacked of proper treatment even for prisoners—felt boots for instance—was banned.

The political prisoners had one thing in common: they were, virtually without exception, innocent of the charges against them. Under a system of terror there is no need for formal charges. To the question of, "What did I do wrong?" comes the answer, "You are from the wrong class," or, "We don't like you." As Solzhenitsyn writes, it was accepted that if one had done nothing, one only got ten years.

What kind of person could be responsible for such a system? Journalists working in the Soviet Union once reported that the Russian press put on a drive to show that Stalin was a human being—on any account a sizeable undertaking. An American correspondent named Barnes managed to visit Stalin's mother, portrayed smiling in her humble cottage, proud of her boy in the Kremlin.[2] The story was widely circulated and surely struck a chord in many a suburban breast.

Stalin was a man obsessed with power, and absolute power corrupted him absolutely (as Nikolai Tolstoi has described in *Stalin's Secret War*). He was the kind of person who could have several portrait artists *shot* because their work displeased him. He could feast on caviar and watch American gangster films while his people were driven to cannibalism. The idolatrous personality cult surrounding him he directed personally, portraying himself as the Wise One from whom all blessings flowed, while at the same time editing entries in the *Great Soviet Encyclopedia* to the effect that Comrade Stalin was "a humble man." In this respect, he maintained all the solid traditions of other Asiatic despots while at the same time surpassing them.

He also shared the traits of other tyrants. His true last name, Dzhugashvili, was long, unusual, and certainly not euphonious. *Hitler* and *Stalin* are more striking than Shickelgruber (the real name of the Führer) and Dzhugashvili. And like Hitler and Napoleon, Stalin was small and from an obscure region, Soviet Georgia. (Hitler was an Austrian and

Napoleon a Corsican.) He spoke Russian with a heavy accent. Like Mao Tse-tung, he came from lowly peasant stock and was not, to put it mildly, of first-rate intelligence, though his cunning made up for this. Doubtless, he also possessed a monumental inferiority complex. Like countless other tyrants, he was the little boy on the block who aspired to be the Big Bully, and when he got his chance he played it to the full. His little finger was thicker than their loins.

This is probably the only true appeal of totalitarian rulers whose works, such as *Mein Kampf, Das Kapital,* and *The Thoughts of Chairman Mao,* are of no real significance other than being another ode to power. Aspiring Third World tyrants are attracted to Marxism for its convenient features of total control and permanent dictatorship. At least until the state fades away.

The best analysis, I believe, of Stalin is to be found in George Orwell's novel *1984.* O'Brien, of the Inner Party, is torturing Winston Smith. He asks him why he thinks the Party commits oppression. Winston replies that they do it for the people's own good. For this erroneous notion, O'Brien sends a jolt of pain into Winston's body, lecturing that the Party does not care about anybody, however loyal, only about power.

I believe that it is not stretching matters to say that Stalin knew that one does not establish a dictatorship to protect a revolution. On the contrary, one makes the revolution in order to establish the dictatorship. For one as sadistic, narrow-minded, paranoid, and vindictive as Stalin, the object of persecution was, simply, persecution; the object of assassination was assassination; and, likewise, the object of cruelty was cruelty. As Milovan Djilas, who knew him, said, there was no crime impossible to Stalin for there was not one he had not committed. He was, Djilas wrote, the greatest criminal in history. Suffice it to say, he represents fallen man at his absolute nadir. To catalog it all would require volumes.

But unlike the case of Hitler, the system founded by Stalin is not part of history. It not only exists today but flourishes and has even been successfully exported. Some current Soviet officials—Andrei Gromyko for instance— served under Stalin himself. The difference between Hitler and Stalin may have been, at one time, limited to the size of their mustaches. But no more.

Another important distinction is that Stalinist regimes require massive military border patrols and such things as the Berlin Wall simply to keep masses of people from fleeing at the first available opportunity. Not even Hitler required this.

The main difference between the two still impinges greatly on the present political debate, particularly in the church. Stalin enjoyed one great, surpassing advantage; he found many influential defenders in the West among clergy, political leaders, and the intelligentsia. Hitler never enjoyed such an illustrious cheering section. For the victims of the arctic death camps, the knowledge that such and such a dignitary in the West supported the man who was working them to death must have been the final indignity. Little wonder that many of them stepped out of line, like Orwell's Winston Smith, welcoming the quick bullet that ended their lives.

Meanwhile, back in the West, the picture of the man in the Kremlin was not that of a bloodthirsty, obscurantist sadist, extreme even by oriental standards, but that of the Good Fabian, the Wise Leader, the Humble Comrade, leading the way to Peace and Happiness forever. The record of Western adulation of this man and his system is truly one of the wonders of all time.

CHAPTER 2, NOTES
1. Robert Conquest, *The Great Terror* (New York: Macmillan, 1968), 699-712.
2. Malcolm Muggeridge, *Chronicles of Wasted Time* (New York: Morrow, 1973), 234.

CHAPTER 3
THE THIRTIES

I put my money on Stalin.   Walter Duranty

This feeling that the Soviet Union is the salvation of the world is growing. I want it to grow more.
        Rev. Hewlett Johnson

One must not make a god of Stalin; he was too valuable for that.   Anna Louise Strong

In the early days of the Soviet Regime, English Fabian socialists Sidney and Beatrice Webb gathered every scrap of information they could find about the USSR and authored the book *Soviet Communism: A New Civilization?* It was only when Stalin began "planning" in earnest that they dropped the question mark from the title. That the planning included the wholesale extermination of large groups of people did not carry a great deal of moral weight. Rather, the leaders were getting things done. But the Webbs were not alone in their assessment.

At the very time when Generalissimo Dzhugashvili terrorized one-sixth of the world, the brightest minds of the West were far from united in condemnation. They did not march in the streets; they burned no Soviet flags, composed no protest songs, and made no films that would be a powerful indictment of what was going on. On the contrary, the Western elite with few exceptions joined in full approval of the man and his regime. Protests were directed against those with the audacity to be anti-Soviet.

Lincoln Steffens returned from the USSR with the famous statement that he had been over to see the future, and it worked. His fellow Americans Theodore Dreiser, Upton Sinclair, John Dos Passos, Walter Duranty, J. Robert Oppenheimer, and others made similar observations.

In Britain, George Bernard Shaw marshalled his oratorical gifts, announcing that Joseph Stalin was subject to dismissal at ten minutes notice if he did not give satisfaction. The Five-Year Plan, Shaw added, was the only hope of the world. Julian Huxley contended that Stalin arose early and helped the workers unload potatoes. Anglican Dean Hewlett Johnson insisted that the masses no more questioned Stalin's tactics than enlightened Britons questioned antiseptic surgery.

In France, artists and poets like Louis Aragon came out with statements to the effect that Stalin was the highest scientific authority in the world, something that would have surprised his countryman Blaise Pascal or even an aspiring scientist like Karl Marx. This occurred at the very time when Stalin, in the best Marxist tradition, championed phonies like the biologist Trofim Lysenko and the gerontologist O.B. Lepeshinskaya, who taught that old age could be forestalled by enemas containing bicarbonate of soda. (It is not known what happened to the lady when it was discovered that her injectable elixir did not work.) André Gide, Romain Rolland, and Jean-Paul Sartre, while not making wild scientific claims for Stalin, nevertheless joined the litany of general adulation.

The Germans too paid tribute, as an examination of the writings of Ernst Toller, Heinrich Mann, Lion Feuchtwanger, and others will verify. In the USSR itself there was Ilya Ehrenburg, Maksim Gorki, and Isaac Babel.

How much of this stuff was there? One could probably measure it in tons, so vast was it. Selecting from this trove, it would be easy to go on multiplying examples of fatuity from all these allegedly keen, critical minds, but this has already been ably and carefully done by other writers.[1]

Of the entire cloud of witnesses to the alleged greatness of Stalin and his regime, two stand out above all the others: an American journalist, Anna Louise Strong, and an English clergyman, Rev. Hewlett Johnson, the Anglican Dean of Canterbury. Both had a religious upbringing. Both roved far and wide, laboring tirelessly. Both, as far as anyone can tell, endured to the end and were thus saved from the unenviable task of admitting that conditions in Workers Paradise were not quite as they had described them.

There is also a human interest story here. At one point, the paths of Johnson and Strong crossed. It is a poignant scene, well worth investigating. But there is a lot of ground to cover first.

CHAPTER 3, NOTES

1. David Caute's *Fellow Travellers: A Postscript to the Enlightenment* concentrates largely on the thirties. Paul Hollander's massive *Political Pilgrims* (1981) deals with the earlier days of the USSR as well as the views of Western intellectuals toward Cuba and China. Both books are thorough, well-documented and eminently readable, though long due to the sheer bulk of the material. That they have not been widely studied is a genuine tragedy, due in part to their high cost. One notes with pleasure that *Political Pilgrims* is now available in paperback.

CHAPTER 4
ANNA LOUISE STRONG

$\mathbf{A}$nna Louise Strong thought most Americans were like her, but she was truly a unique person. In fact, there has never been anyone quite like her anywhere, nor is there likely to be, despite some spirited attempts. Her life would be excellent film fodder, but Hollywood moguls have shown no interest. Her story is, ultimately, better left unfilmed since characters on the screen all too often bear scant resemblance to their counterparts in the real world. And in her case that would be a genuine shame.

Strong's inclusion here is not, I should hasten to add, due to any quota system or tokenism. On the contrary, she was chosen because she surpassed many of her male contemporaries. For Anna Louise Strong equality was not an issue. She led the field.

The future author of works with titles like *I Change Worlds* was born in Friend, Nebraska in 1885. Her ancestry in North America went back to the arrival of one John Strong in Massachusetts in 1630. Her grandmother's sister, Lizzie Lord, married President Benjamin Harrison. Of her forebearers she wrote:

> They had faith that humanity inevitably advances with
> each generation and that new things are usually best.[1]

In more ways then one, Anna strictly adhered to the faith of her predecessors. Sydney Strong, her father, was a minister in the Congregationalist denomination. She remembers him fondly as a man who almost followed the ethics of Jesus.

Rev. Strong got into trouble defending Darwin and preaching against war. It is reasonable to assume that if he, like his daughter, had equated the ethics of Jesus with a platitude like "the greatest good for the greatest number"[2] that this would also have drawn criticism from the deacons and elders. Anna likened him to Tolstoy but it is not known if he wrote. His jottings on Anna's enthusiasms and travels might make interesting reading.

Anna's mother met Sydney at Oberlin College. Among the precepts these educated parents taught their daughter was to avoid all unpleasant things, to the point that she disbelieved evil right before her eyes.[3] Judging by the amount of evil she was to both witness then subsequently ignore in her life, her parents taught her well.

Anna finished her first eight years of school in four. She briefly studied languages in Germany and Switzerland then spent two years at Bryn Mawr. She completed studies at Oberlin College in 1905 then moved on to the University of Chicago, graduating magna cum laude. Anna Louise became not only the youngest person to ever receive a doctorate from the institution—she was 23—but the first woman ever to do so. Her thesis was titled, "A Study of Prayer From The Standpoint of Social Psychology." The University of Chicago Press published the dissertion as a book.

Between her graduate and postgraduate studies, Strong became associate editor of *Advance*, a fundamentalist (her adjective) weekly published in Chicago. She labored prodigiously, writing under several pseudonyms. Her work for *Advance* included, of all things, fairy tales, of which she was to author more than a few in her long life. She was fired for unspecified reasons after five months, something she compared to rape.[4]

Anna was to move from fundamentalism to socialism in Kansas City, where she worked on the Child Welfare Exhibit. Apparently she had been given some management responsibilities and was forced to lay off a young draftsman. It became a spiritual-political experience:

> The world was horrible chaos, insecure. Not one of the reforms I had ever been told about would fix it; I tried them all that night. The only remedy would be a world quite differently organized, where work and jobs and wages were public matters, and everything that condition them was publicly owned, where society organized assignment of work and cut everybody's hours to fit work and looked after all workers and all children learning to work and all old people after their work was done. That was common sense; it was efficiency; it was abolition of chaos and waste. I knew enough to know that such a society was called socialism, and that I must be a socialist.[5]

It is not clear just how Anna "tried all the reforms she had ever heard about" in one night, but her strategy became clear. The draftsman in question should not have sought other work, or relocated, or undertaken further studies. Neither, in her view, was the American system capable any longer of change as it had been in the past, according to her own admission. No programs or incentives could now be implemented to remedy the situation. No, none of this would work. The draftsman should not change; rather, the world would have to change. The new world would have to be socialist. Anna became one.

Moving to Seattle, she got involved with the labor movement (specifically, with the International Workers of the World) and served on the local school board. Her overseas efforts began with the Friends Services Committee. She went to the Soviet Union in the early twenties.

Though she never joined the Communist party, the Russian revolution drew her like a magnet draws filings. Did she actually study Marx and Lenin? In one of the few confessions she makes (had not her father and mother told her to be right in her soul?) she admits:

> I began to think of Marx. I had avoided reading him because
> he always aroused my desire to look on all sides of the ques-
> tion and I could admire the Russian communists better when
> I didn't read their theories.[6]

Anyone in Miss Strong's position must always be vigi-
lant against seeing all sides of a question—even if this means
shunning Karl Marx. Anna remained, in principle, rigorously onesided.

Of all the early newspaper correspondents in Moscow,
Strong, Louis Fischer, and the *New York Times*'s man Walter
Duranty adhered most carefully to every shift of the party
line. Strong actually edited the *Moscow News*, an English-
language Soviet publication for American readership. This
placed her in the position of a propagandist, which, of
course, she was. Her books and books critical of her are full of
examples, but some stand out as worthy of special mention.

Soviet prisons especially interested Western social
planners and reformers. Specially trained guides led the
eager troops on tours of selected institutions, hardly typical
of Soviet jails but convincing at least to Bernard Shaw. He
described the system as so benevolent that prisoners had to
be induced to leave.[7] On any score, this is hard to top, but
Anna Louise Strong was not about to be outdone. She
claimed that under conditions in Socialism criminals actually applied to prisons for admittance![8]

Reports from Anna followed a pattern: turnip produc-
tion in the Ukraine is up 35 percent, learned, first-hand articles would say. How did she know? She didn't, but it mat-
tered little to those who read the news. The bogus statistics
passed on into the lore of the time, the materialist equivalent
of splinters of the true cross.

Anna married Joel Shurbin, a Russian agronomist, but
he died ten years later; they had no children, leaving her free
to travel.

And travel she did. Strong voyaged far and wide promoting the Soviet Union to which she had dedicated every
fiber of her being. So complete was her dedication that when

Stalin decreed it was high time not to merely limit the kulaks but to *abolish them as a class*, Anna described it this way:

> Stalin had merely analyzed and authorized what farm-hands were already instinctively doing.[9]

She might have written that Hitler had only authorized what individual racists were already instinctively doing, or that Mao merely authorized what the zealous Red Guards were instinctively doing. For her part, Anna knew very well not only what was going on but what she herself was doing: deceiving editors and the Western public. She wrote that it amused her to see how much she could put over.[10]

One might say that she did it instinctively well for she was able to "put over" a great deal, including various versions of the following.

> One must not make a god of Stalin; he was too valuable for that. He analyzed the mechanical and human forces out of which gods arose and died. Not Stalin, but the will of the working class which Stalin analyzed, had thrown out Trotsky. . . . I had seen the brains of communists give at last a line and a name to it, till the Five Year Plan burst forth from the loins of a hundred and sixty million people, who were tortured by a thousand compromises, clamorous for the pains of birth.[11]

Here Anna strays back to her genre of the fairy tale: a Plan bursting forth from the loins of the multitudes; Prince Stalin and his analytical mind, beseiged by the rapacious two-headed dragon of Trotsky and the Capitalist Past, not to mention the trollish, grasping kulaks. All that remained for the tale was that all parties should live happy, planned lives forever. As it turned out, the people clamored for more than the pains of birth and were tortured with more than compromises.

The few journalists who attempted—in spite of heavy censorship—to tell the truth did not, to say the least, regard Anna Louise highly. Malcolm Muggeridge, in fact, once found himself seated on a couch between Anna Louise and Louis Fischer.

> Miss Strong was an enormous woman with a very red face, a
> lot of white hair, and an expression of stupidity so over-
> whelming that it amounted to a kind of strange beauty. [12]

This is not just a gratuitous physical attack. Peoples'
mental activity can indeed affect the very way they look,
their countenance. Rock stars, for example, tend to get an
emaciated, ethereal look. Television addicts contract a certain blank stare. It is entirely consistent and logical that Miss
Strong should appear stupid to Mr. Muggeridge. In view of
her concealment of Stalin's murderous crimes, stupid might
even be kind.

In spite of all her faithful service, Anna was to discover
that the great dictatorship of the proletariat can turn without
warning on its most servile toadies. In 1949, the GPU (now
the KGB) tossed her without warning into Lubianka prison.
Unlike the eager Soviet criminals she wrote about, she had
not even applied for admission. They interrogated her for
five days. It may be farfetched, but it would be nice to think
that some day the transcripts of these sessions would be made
public, perhaps if the Soviet government enacts a Freedom
of Information Act based on the American model. But no
one should hold his breath.

Muggeridge reports that news of Strong's arrest elicited
much joy among old Moscow hands who had known her.
Some even sent congratulatory telegrams to the Soviet government. But they didn't keep her long. Muggeridge speculates that even in prison she proved tedious. The GPU un-
ceremoniously dumped her into Poland.

Fortunately, Anna had kept her U.S. citizenship and
passport—just in case. One can never be too careful. Back in
America, she spilled it all to the bourgeois, capitalist *New
York Herald Tribune*. Fellow travelers like Corliss Lamont
shared her outrage. And after all the lies she had cheerfully
written for them! Defending genocide even! What kind of
gratitude was this?

She may have, like the imbecilic Parsons in Orwell's
1984, maintained that the party had somehow made a mis-

take. And they had. Some years later the Soviet government cleared Strong of any lingering spy accusations. (Is this the only time the Soviet dictatorship of the proletariat has admitted wrong? It is not impossible.)

Now interrogation by the GPU cannot be a pleasant experience. One would think that the episode would have been just what Anna needed, a mugging by reality, as it were, capable of unleashing her considerable powers of indignation. But other than the one article, it was not to be. A lover's quarrel would best describe it. Jilted by Stalin, she turned to another.

Like a groupie who offers her favors to rock bands, Strong went to China. There she defended or denied the Great Helmsman's purges, crimes, "progress," and dogmas as stridently as she had ever done in Russia. It must be remembered that Anna was "motor-minded" and only knew why she had acted after the fact. Some inner cruise control kept her going; some mysterious, illogical gyroscope kept her on course.

Mao Tse-tung knew a good thing when he saw it. No, there would be no midnight arrests, no interrogations in his domains—at least not for Miss Strong. He set her up in the capital with special accommodations and a staff. For her part, she propagandized faithfully in her publication *Letter From China.* Mao was, effectively, her new editor. She swam and dined with the Master who, in great benevolence, made her an honorary Red Guard during the Cultural Revolution. Upon receiving this title, did she breathe an awestruck thank-you speech?—"I would like to thank my parents, who taught me to ignore evil." Did she shed a few tears over this great honor? It would be nice to think so.

Strong never returned to the United States. She died in Peking in 1970. Mao conferred full canonization by according her a state funeral.

Intrepid souls who care to investigate Anna's most interesting life will discover that the human potential for falsification is bottomless, however many letters follow the name and whether or not the graduation was, like Anna's, magna cum laude. Though Strong bore no children, her spiritual descendants are many. What is worse, many of the myths she perpetrated are alive and well. She is forgotten, but not gone.

CHAPTER 4, NOTES
  1. Anna Louise Strong, *I Change Worlds* (New York: Holt, 1935), 5.
  2. Ibid., 6.
  3. Ibid., 16.
  4. Ibid., 29.
  5. Ibid., 40-41.
  6. Ibid., 384.
  7. George Bernard Shaw, *Rationalization of Russia*, 91.
  8. Paul Hollander, *Political Pilgrims* (New York: Oxford University Press, 1981), 146.
  9. Strong, *I Change Worlds*, 289.
  10. Ibid., 224.
  11. Ibid., 348.
  12. Malcolm Muggeridge, *Chronicles of Wasted Time* (New York: Morrow, 1973), 1:254.

CHAPTER 5
THE VERY REVEREND HEWLETT JOHNSON, DEAN OF CANTERBURY

Prototalitarian clergymen are a decidedly modern phenomenon. The early Christians, with all their glaring faults, never produced anyone capable of seeing in Alaric, the Visigoth king who sacked Rome, the coming savior of the world. Modern tyrants, however, compared to whom Alaric was a bumbling and squeamish amateur, have had many enthusiastic supporters in the pulpit. If some sort of hall of fame were to be constructed for these clergy, the Very Reverend Hewlett Johnson, Dean of Canterbury, would surely be inducted on the first ballot.

Born in 1874 at Kersal, near Manchester, Johnson was brought up in religious surroundings, but his clerical aspirations did not become manifest until much later. He studied engineering at Victoria University. Here he reported that the teaching of Darwinian evolution dealt the beliefs of his youth a shock from which he never recovered. But he maintained interest in Christianity and at one time aspired to use his engineering talents on the mission field. This concept was also popular in the seventies in the United States, so the Reverend Johnson may be said to have been ahead of his time not only in the field of apologizing for totalitarian dictatorships but in the realm of missions as well.

During his early engineering work in England, various socialists practiced their brand of personal evangelism on young Hewlett, witnessing to him while working at their lathes. He fell under deep conviction. His salary amounted to a scant thirteen shillings a week, but he experienced guilt over his conditions of alleged comfort. Although he may have been the only one who ever tried, he "could not equate business with Christianity."[1] Later in his life, however, when the business was a five-year plan and the entrepreneur Joseph Stalin, he had no problem with the equation.

About this time Johnson received a missionary call. The missionary society requested that he undertake additional theological studies, so he enrolled at a Wadnaw College, a divinity school associated with Oxford. Here, Johnson wrote, "Literary and historical criticism and philosophy completed what evolutionary teaching had begun and gave a new release of thought."[2] He graduated in 1900 with a degree in theology, but the missionary society to which he had applied now found him unsuitable. But though this door had been closed, a stained-glass window opened. The Church of England had work for him.

They ordained Johnson and installed him as a vicar in a fairly affluent suburb. His socialist views were so well known that he was rejected as a chaplain during World War I. It is tempting to see in his two rejections—as a chaplain and a missionary—the source for Johnson's later championing of those dedicated to the destruction of Britain, but revenge was surely not his motive. David Caute in *Fellow Travellers* writes of Johnson as an amiable and polite man, Christian in deportment if not exactly strong on doctrine. Socialism was his orthodoxy, and he believed fervently in its inerrancy. He described Jesus as a "materialist" and saw socialism as the fulfillment of Christianity. He wrote during the thirties, "Herr Hitler is clear-headed enough to see that Judaism and Christianity provide the high road to socialism and communism."[3]

From 1913 to 1924 Johnson served as examining chaplain to the bishops of Exeter. In addition, in 1919, he was

made honorary canon of Chester Cathedral. In 1926 he became select preacher at Cambridge and finally, in 1931, by
appointment of King George the Fifth, Dean of Canterbury.
From this lofty post he made statements such as this:

> Communism has recovered the essential form of a real belief
> in God which organized Christianity just now has largely
> lost.[4]

His continued socialist afflatus garnered him the tag, "the
Red Dean."

Even after the Nazi-Soviet pact, Johnson continued to
support the USSR. He was referred to by men of like sentiments as a prophetic "voice crying in the wilderness," a
"moral bridge between Russia and England." He wrote for
the *Daily Worker* and authored a book, *The Socialist Sixth of
the Earth*, which even then drew negative reviews. W. H.
Chamberlain in the *Saturday Review* spoke of its "complete
factual vacuum" adding that Johnson's version bore no more
resemblance to the real USSR than the Beatitudes did to
Mein Kampf.[5] In his own country, the *Manchester Guardian*
mused, "One wonders reading the Dean's book whether he
has any critical sense left at all."[6] Observing the Dean's life,
one wonders whether he ever had any critical sense to begin
with. But the book enjoyed an enormous sale in spite of these
reviewers, who might have been the real voices crying in the
wilderness.

Johnson, for his part, hit full stride. He was a striking
figure in robes and gaiters, tall, spare, and bald, with tufts of
white hair above the ears. In 1942 he told a mass meeting in
Liverpool, "This feeling that the Soviet Union is the salvation of the world is growing. I want it to grow more."[7]
Though he affirmed the moral and economic superiority of
Soviet socialism over Western capitalism, this did not stop
him from requesting donations for "peace" causes from rich
capitalists, particularly film stars. Stalin's response was to
award Rev. Johnson the—what else?—Stalin Peace prize in
1951.

Was there no opposition to Johnson from within the Church? Certainly, but the gentle Dean gave no quarter and prevailed. In a sense, he had a government job. The toiling masses could take comfort in the fact that at least one member of the Church of England hierarchy was on the side of history, peace, and progress.

Johnson's writings about the Soviet Union are alternately tedious and infuriating, but some of his observations cannot go unmentioned. Those who write will perhaps appreciate this insight into artistic freedom.

> To understand and appreciate the situation as the Soviet People themselves see it, we must remember that much which we call liberty Russia would call license, and that Russia in general accepts the communist creed in precisely the same way as we accept modern science. The public no more questions the communist creed than we question antiseptic surgery. The Communist Party feel they have as much right to recall artists to their faith as to recall a doctor who disregarded antisepsis in his surgery. They protest by criticism and persuasion, not by sending the artist to Siberia. Nor do Soviet literary men themselves resent the criticism. What in reality we see is the whole literary world putting its house in order. The people as a whole also resented the easygoing attitude of literary men who uttered no protest against what they knew was evil writing.[8]

And what about that nasty accusation that the Soviet Union was an expansionist state? That business about Eastern Europe and the tiny, trifling Baltic states of Latvia, Lithuania, and Estonia?

> It should hardly be necessary when one considers the facts, to meet the charge that Russia is expansionist, were the charge less persistent. These are the facts. During the war, and largely through military necessity, the Baltic states, a small part of Finland, Bessarabia, the country east of the "Curzon Line" and a small fragment of East Prussia have been incorporated. With the exception of the last small item all this was part of Russia at the time of the Revolution and with the exception of the Baltic peoples all were of Russian or near-Russian stock.[9]

Notice and appreciate the clever euphemism of "incorporated" for "taken over," as though it were a matter for a city council meeting. Also the "military necessity." That pretty well wrapped it up as far as the Dean was concerned. And anyway, were not all these areas once part of the Russian Empire? The argument has been used many times by many apologists: wherever the czars ruled, the dictatorship of the proletariat has a right to rule as well; this in spite of the crowings for self-determination. Then too there is the business of "near-Russian stock." In other words, "they are like us, we can therefore take them over." But the Reverend Johnson is merely endorsing Pan-Slavism here. He quickly moves on to compare this alleged expansion with the acquisitions of the United States, which turn out to be air bases in various countries and assistance to others. He tops this off with the ludicrous charge that the United States controls three-quarters of the world (Really? India? China? All the colonial and liberated African states?) before dropping the subject entirely. Elsewhere he answers the question, Is the Soviet Union a force for peace? by quoting Stalin's "historic speech" of 1939, which begins with "We stand for peace." Stalin said it, Johnson believed it, and that was that. For the Dean of Canterbury, no doubt existed that a speech by Stalin would not cure.

Johnson, in fact, met Stalin, whom he constantly refers to as "The Generalissimo," thus unintentionally providing his most accurate description of the Wise Leader. They spoke for about an hour in the Kremlin. Johnson's account provides a few unintended laughs. But his conclusion is no joke:

> No man of mystery dominates the Kremlin. Stalin is the embodiment of good-humored common sense, as much a man of the people today as when he plied the secret printing press in the commonplace villa in Tbilisi. . . . Stalin I found exactly like the speeches he had uttered through a quarter of a century as mouthpiece of the new Soviet Order. . . . A man, furthermore, who seeks friendship with Britain and believes in its possibility.[10]

The peace-loving Dean broke character in attacking Arthur Koestler and other anti-Soviet writers whom he contemptuously labeled, "the disillusioned class." These "crude" people had the nerve to call into question the violent means—genocide for instance—used to attain allegedly beneficial ends. Johnson's efforts to straighten this out will be of interest to all students of casuistry. Particularly this gem:

> Those who shrink from such lengths of the absolutist position still find in non-violence a Western and Christian virtue and use its non-observance in the stern events of Russia in the last quarter of a century as a stick with which to beat the Soviet Union, pointing to the violence of its early days: the death of the Tsar, the elimination of the Kulaks, the ruthlessness of the purges. Russia's answer to these charges would probably run as follows:
>
> You, they would say, were determined at all costs, with violence if need be, to prevent Hitler from putting the shackles on your hands and your children's hands. You would sacrifice millions of lives to prevent it. Why then, take a high moral platform and preach at us, who at the cost of a few thousand lives, and only by that cost, were enabled to shake off similar shackles which for centuries had crippled our ancestors and now us?
>
> Then, the idealists would say, you justify the wrong?
>
> By no means, they would reply. To call it wrong again is to beg the question. The rightness or wrongness of any act must be judged by its whole context and consequences. In the light of its context it would not be wrong.[11]

This may be the most cavalier defense of genocide—he acknowledges that the kulaks were "eliminated"—in history. The Dean goes on to compare Lenin and Christ. There is much, much more of the same. But why go on?

Johnson pressed ever onward. He traveled widely through Eastern Europe and even went to Cuba. At the age of *ninety*, he toured China at the behest of Cho En-lai. Imagine his surprise when in Peking he met up with, yes, soulmate Anna Louise Strong. It was a meeting made in utopia, a geriatric *Reds*. Did Anna reveal details of her brief visit to Lubianka prison? Had she done so—and I think she did—

the Dean would undoubtedly have, in deepest sympathy, trotted out his strongest term of criticism for the Soviet Union, calling their treatment of her a "blunder." What a pity that their conversation is lost forever. Imagine them swapping stories, comparing notes, perhaps even pausing for a word of prayer. They surely helped to bolster each other's faith and exhort each other to continued good works.

Johnson died two years later, in 1966. He did not live to see Soviet socialism surpass the West and was doubtless disappointed at not being on location when the state withered away. His apologetic skills were sorely missed by the Kremlin during the invasions of Czechoslovakia and Afghanistan, and certainly by Mao during the Cultural Revolution, though perhaps Anna Louise filled in for him, capable as she was in that capacity. Sadly, Johnson did not have the opportunity to call Solzhenitsyn a liar for revealing the realities of the gulag. Indeed, the country he viewed as the salvation of mankind now claims few foreign admirers. Hence, in many senses, Johnson was a personal and professional failure. His life is best captured in a vignette from his postwar trip to Russia.

> A short, thick-set man with a broad, good-humored, highly intelligent face stepped easily in front of the grand piano, and placing on his forefingers two india-rubber balls the size of tennis balls, painted to resemble human faces, he conducted a miniature pantomime. Fingers entirely unrobed magically assumed the role of bodies, arms and legs, as Mr. Andriyevish the magician, who had founded Moscow's famous puppet theater, depicted love, passion, joy despair, and "all lived happily ever afterwards."[12]

Johnson wrote that the incident stood out vividly in his memory. Perhaps for him it was a parable of the role he played for Stalin, a most effective, inexpensive, and surely sometimes amusing puppet. But the Generalissimo, in spite of his open loathing of Western "rotten liberals" did not let Johnson's years of toil pass unnoticed or uncompensated.

In fact, Johnson stands as a monument to just how

highly totalitarian dictators, particularly mass murderers, value the services of apologetic clergymen or, if you will, liberation theologians. After all, these people give them free access to the very minds and consciences of Western Christians. How valuable is this service?

In the *Great Soviet Encyclopedia*, the entry for the Very Reverend Hewlett Johnson, Dean of Canterbury, is longer than the one for Jesus Christ. Verily I say unto you, he had his reward.

CHAPTER 5, NOTES
1. *Current Biography* (New York: Wilson, 1943), 350.
2. Ibid.
3. Ibid.
4. Ibid., 351.
5. W. H. Chamberlain, quoted in *Current Biography*, 351.
6. *The Manchester Guardian*, quoted in *Current Biography*, 351.
7. *Current Biography*, 351.
8. Hewlett Johnson, *Soviet Russia Since the War* (Westport, Conn.: Greenwood Press, 1979), 115.
9. Ibid., 255.
10. Ibid., 72.
11. Ibid., 262.
12. Ibid., 15.

CHAPTER 6
LEGACY

The reasons for the cult of the Stalin regime in the West go back, as David Caute contends, to the Enlightenment. As Koestler remarked, since that time the place of God has been vacant with Reason, and by extension Man, ruling in his place. It was no longer God's law but man's that prevailed. And man himself was no longer viewed as a being created in the image and likeness of God but, rather, the product of a long process of evolution. This deification of man is a subterranean stream in the Western tradition. In the thirties it surfaced with radical consequences when the general concept centered on one man—Stalin.

Another legacy of the Enlightenment was the view that the major incarnation of Rationality was Science. This goes back to Saint-Simon and his École Polytechnique.[1] The Soviet Union came to be viewed as a society organized on the highest scientific principles, not because this was true but because the regime and its foreign supporters said it was. Credulity did the rest, along with circumstances. The Western, capitalistic world at the time seemed to be coming apart at the seams with depression, unrest, war. At this point the first scientific society appears, headed by an acclaimed Great Leader. Now who could resist that?

In the USSR, mankind, reduced by prevailing theories to just another biological species, was being transformed. Human nature itself was being changed—so the line went. One frequently comes across references to Soviet society as a "great experiment"; its scientific elite and the ruling powers united in being and purpose, with nothing to hinder them from tinkering with their vast human laboratory.

Scientists and intellectuals in the West shared this vision of the scientist-king (viz. themselves) with "superior brains," planning the ignorant, religious, and selfish masses into the Future with, of course, their steady consent and occasional thunderous applause. But the trouble was, in their own societies they lacked opportunity.

Free societies, where people largely do as they please, are not the best milieu for those who derive their significance from directing, exhorting, and tutoring others or, as Eric Hoffer put it, minding other people's business. Teachers, reformers, planners, and clergy fit this description.

Free societies do not accord superior status to such an idea-hierarchy as does the closed scientific model. Just about anyone has the potential to make it and earn wealth or prestige. This does not sit well with those who possess social blueprints. They are openly resentful. Thus the open society is as much a threat to the academic and idea-elite's sense of worth as a society of robots would be to a working man's worth. There is a direct link between adherence to scientific determinism and the rejection of a free and open society. That people are free to ignore them (something they frequently do) infuriates the academic, social planner, or clergyman with a sweeping agenda. One can monitor this by the number of times the question "What kind of society is this?" is raised about democracy, or diatribes are intoned against individualism, or the common person, for whom the elitist is allegedly compassionate, is scorned as one in the grip of imbecile enthusiasms and shallow consumerism.

What is actually being attacked is the principle that people should be free not only to ignore the views of an elite often isolated from the populace at large and steeped in a world of pure theory, but free also to propagate their idea of personal liberty and the political agenda that makes this the primary objective of government.

With much of the elite in the West thus constrained during the thirties, it was only natural that the USSR should seem like a social engineer's paradise. There the planners, as long as they held to scientific socialism, were veritable gods. Those recalcitrant masses could be *forced* by naked police power to do what was good for them. They could be relocated where they were needed ("from each according to his ability"). They could be taught first hand just what altruism was all about ("to each according to his need").

The existence of a government thus committed to social change, which did not allow outdated moral considerations—or even the lives of mere people—to get in the way, caused many members of the Western elite to swoon with delight. They proceeded to savagely denigrate their own countries and praise the USSR and its ruler Stalin with a sycophancy seldom, if ever, equalled.[2] (There are other reasons for the appeal of totalitarian regimes in the West, especially to the church. They will be dealt with later.)

Today, even in the USSR, few disagree that the early planning involved terrorism, famine, and death on a massive scale. It was, like the entire Soviet experiment, a *failure*. And in the materialist Marxist state, evil and failure are the same thing. To put it as plainly as possible, those Western teachers, writers, philanthropists, and clergy who so readily gave their blessing were *wrong*. Few came forward to say so. However, there were some.

CHAPTER 6, NOTES
1. For a treatment of the subject see F. A. Hayek's *The Counterrevolution of Science*.
2. The record is open for examination in *Fellow Travellers*, *Political Pilgrims*, and other works such as *The Opium of the Intellectuals* by Raymond Aron.

SECTION 2
DISSENT

One positive footnote to the whole tragicomic chapter of human history is that there have been some former partisans who were honest enough to admit their errors. Considering the intellectual climate of the time, this took great courage.

But while apologists like Sartre have gone from strength to strength, multiplying the species like rabbits, this group has largely been ignored. One cannot touch on them all, but there are select cases that cry out to be heard.

They are an eclectic bunch—an American, a Quebecois, two Englishmen, a Hungarian, and a Yugoslav. They range from news correspondents to all-purpose scribes to Nobel laureates; from former disc jockeys to the former vice president of a Marxist European country. It will be noticed that their paths sometimes crossed and that some of them knew each other.

Of the entire group, I have allowed myself the liberty of quoting Malcolm Muggeridge more than any of the others since he is the only one with whom I have had personal contact. There are other reasons, though, which should be clear by the end of the book.

What all these people have in common is that, unlike so many worshipers from afar, they actually *lived* under Marxist socialism in one form or another, whether in the USSR, Cuba, or Yugoslavia. They differed from the comfy defenders of totalitarianism found in peerages and among tenured professors in that Marxism was not, for them, an intellectual hobby. No, socialist *countries* with real people and defined borders actually existed. They went there to see for themselves. The experience changed them forever.

CHAPTER 7
MALCOLM MUGGERIDGE

Malcolm Muggeridge has always loved words and from his youth never doubted that they were his métier. Perhaps taking note of this, his parents gave him a toy printing set on which he produced his first composition. The story was about a train that raced along, speeding past all stations. This pleased those passengers whose destinations lay further along the line, but their delight soon turned to rage when they realized the train was not going to stop at their stations either. The train sped inexorably on, out of their control. Muggeridge reports that the tale practically wrote itself and that he had no idea what, if anything, it meant. But after years of, as he once told his father, fighting out the struggles of life on paper, it has become clear: it was the same story he has been writing ever since—the story of our time.

Born in 1903, Muggeridge spans the century over which, as a writer, he has maintained a careful watch in what he calls his journalistic power-voyeur role. Few other writers can match his experience or output, not to mention his depth, but his writing is hardly limited to journalism.

Three Flats, his first play, was produced by the State Society of London. He has also written fiction, *Autumnal Face; Winter in Moscow; Affairs of the Heart;* and *In a Valley of This*

Restless Mind. Another novel, *Picture Palace*, about a liberal newspaper in the north of England, had to be withdrawn when the *Guardian*—the obvious model for the story and a passionate advocate of freedom of speech—threatened a libel suit.

Absorbing this heavy blow, Muggeridge wrote on, authoring, among other works, *The Thirties* and *The Earnest Atheist: A Life of Samuel Butler.* His autobiography, *Chronicles of Wasted Time*, recounts among other things his stint in Moscow, his espionage experiences in Mozambique during World War II, and his work as a liaison officer in postwar France. For his achievements in the latter two areas, he received the *Legion d'Honneur* and the *Croix de Guerre*.

All his life Muggeridge has wrestled with the question of the meaning of life but only began to write overtly religious books in the late sixties. These include *Jesus Rediscovered; A Third Testament; The End of Christendom; Christ and the Media; Things Past; Jesus the Man Who Lives*; and *Something Beautiful for God*, the story of Mother Teresa of Calcutta. It should be added that although these are religious books, they are quite unlike the great majority of works in that category or, for that matter, unlike just about anything else. This will be immediately apparent to the new reader.

Neither have Muggeridge's television documentaries been typical of religious broadcasting. Although he has often appeared on television (his first assignment was to interview Billy Graham), he dislikes the medium and never watches it himself, something he calls the moral equivalent of a prostate operation.

The preceeding is, of course, only the briefest sketch of a multifaceted man who, as I have discovered, is scarcely known in North America other than as an eloquent foe of abortion, or a new member of the Roman Catholic church, or, perhaps in rare cases, the former editor of the British humor magazine *Punch.* One would love to launch into a full treatment of his life, but this has already been done by Ian Hunter in *Malcolm Muggeridge, A Life.*

By way of tribute, I have found in Malcolm Muggeridge a trusty Sherpa guide as I've wandered on the peaks and crags of this shaky century. He is one who knows the paths; he has been there before. This is particularly true on the question of socialism in which faith, like him, I was brought up. But this dimension of his life, including his experiences in Russia, is generally unknown in America.

Harry Muggeridge, Malcolm's father, was a pioneer socialist of the Fabian persuasion. (The group took its name from Fabius, a Roman reformer committed to peaceful, gradual change.) The Fabians expected a better world just around the corner, ushered in by moderate men of all shades of opinion prevailing through the ballot box, then peacefully nationalizing everything and everyone until the State, Producer, and Consumer were united in a new trinity, leading to an era of peace and cooperation forever.

Malcolm's father ran for Parliament, and his son campaigned for him vigorously, going door to door informing people that a vote for his father was a vote for a better world. They held street corner meetings in the manner of the Salvation Army, and the socialist Sunday school Malcolm attended even passed a collection plate, though according to its doctrines money was as dangerous a substance as heroin. The Muggeridge household jostled with Fabians, utopians, sympathetic clergy, and such famous persons as Bernard Shaw and H. G. Wells.

The elder Muggeridge tried to edit Malcolm into a version of himself and was successful in that his son shared his political ideas. Indeed, Malcolm possessed every advantage for a brilliant socialist career. Arthur Koestler described his own life as an arrow in the blue, a quest for infinity. Malcolm's was a search for the Green Stick. (The reference is to Tolstoy who fancied that somewhere lay buried a green stick on which words were carved that would destroy the evil in the hearts of men and bring them everything good.) Both Koestler and Muggeridge were to wind up—temporarily—in the same utopia.

After spending four years at Cambridge, it was off to a teaching position in India. Here he corresponded with and met Mahatma Gandhi. Later, teaching in Egypt, he began to write about the twilight of British imperialism for the *Manchester Guardian*.

Back in England, when the suggestion came that he should replace the *Guardian's* Moscow correspondent, Muggeridge jumped at the chance. Not only the British Empire but British civilization itself he considered moribund. In the USSR, he imagined, he would be part of a state that had a future, whereas Britain and the West had only a past. In addition, Malcolm had excellent references: his wife's relatives, Sidney and Beatrice Webb, authors of *Soviet Communism: A New Civilization*, were highly respected in the Soviet Union, as was the *Manchester Guardian*.

Malcolm and his wife Kitty cheerfully burned their bridges. They disposed of such trivia as diplomas and marriage certificates which they considered relics of bourgeois servitude. They hoped their second child would be born in Russia and become a Soviet citizen. In the summer of 1932, the venerable Webbs saw them off. They set sail on the good ship *Kooperatsia*.

There were surely doubts in Malcolm's mind before the start of this his, as he imagined, last adventure, and very soon the alarm bells started ringing. At one port of call the ship's doctor came aboard drunk, a shock to Malcolm who thought that socialist doctors should not get drunk like capitalist ones. This was only one incident, but it indicates that, at the time, he was so unsettled that he wrote the following in his diary on his first day in Moscow:

> Today I arrived in Moscow. Already I have made up my mind to call this the *Diary of a Journalist* and not the *Diary of a Communist*. Moscow is an exquisite city. All the time I alternate between complete despair and wild hope. Walking by the Kremlin, and seeing the Red Flag float over the golden domes, I reflected that what made the revolution so attractive to a certain type of person was that, like revivalist religion, it exalts the humble and meek.[1]

Muggeridge found the job of correspondent easy enough; after all, there was only one source of information. News had been nationalized. One simply had to select an item from the Soviet press, write it up in a form suitable for foreign consumption, and get it passed by the censors. This was not always easy. The Soviet bosses at that time were able to control foreign newsmen almost as much as their own by threatening the withdrawal of visas or, where this failed, using sterner measures. Checking the accuracy of government statistics was impossible, hence many journalists freely embellished their accounts, falsifying what was already false.

One can well imagine that the true statistics were quite different if they were known at all. One government censor, Oumansky, told Muggeridge on one occasion that he couldn't write a certain story because it was true. In a similar vein, around the time of the trials of the early Bolsheviks, the word was that "everything was true but the facts."

Censors could be avoided by sending stories via the diplomatic bag. Malcolm did this once and received a tongue lashing and threats from Oumansky for his trouble. He had written on the subject of the Soviet mania for seeing agents provocateurs behind every rock and tree, comparing this to Voltaire's statement about God—that if he did not exist it would be necessary to invent him. Muggeridge was not among the "objective" (double-speak for "most obedient to the party") journalists such as Walter Duranty, Maurice Hindus, and Anna Louise Strong who followed the slightest shift of the party line. This shift, as in the case of the Nazi-Soviet pact, often became not only a lurch but a complete about-face. But they followed it all the same, and the Western masses, for the most part, accepted their accounts as gospel. Duranty, one of the worst of the bunch, gained a reputation as a Soviet expert.

> By the same token, if the *New York Times* went on all those years giving great prominence to Duranty's messages when they were so evidently nonsensically untrue, to the point that he came to be accepted as the great Russian expert

in America, and played a major part in shaping President Roosevelt's policies vis-à-vis the USSR. This was not, we may be sure, because the *Times* was deceived. Rather, because it wanted to be so deceived, and Duranty provided the requisite deception material. Since his time, there have been a whole succession of others fulfilling the same role—in Cuba, in Vietnam, in Latin America. It is an addiction, and in such cases there is never any lack of hands to push in the needle and give the fix. Just as the intelligentsia have been foremost in the struggle to abolish intelligence, so the great organs of capitalism like the *New York Times* have spared no expense to ensure that capitalism will not survive.[2]

Nothing can substitute for Muggeridge's own description of these people and experiences as recorded in the first volume of his autobiography, *The Green Stick*, and in the novel *Winter in Moscow*. (The latter book, to Malcolm's great delight, circulated in *samizdat* form in the USSR and may circulate still.) Some brief citations from Muggeridge's diaries indicate how he saw the entire situation.

It was often claimed of the USSR and other Marxist states that they were based on cooperation in contrast to the vicious competition of the West. Malcolm saw the base of the USSR quite differently:

> When class hatred flares up in you, only then is Marxism intelligible. Not necessarily admirable, but intelligible. Soviet society is based on the lust of class hatred. Theoretically it is also based on the public school of classlessness. So now I see more than ever the meaning of class conflicts.[3]

Many of the early sympathizers with the USSR were pacifists. Refusing to serve in the armies of their own countries and opposing any military action by their respective governments, they changed their stance where class warfare was concerned. Perhaps they were only, like Hewlett Johnson, 90 percent pacifist, though in his case, through that other 10 percent, entire Soviet military parades could goose step with complete safety. Muggeridge reports that pacifists and representatives from the peace churches fairly swooned when the tanks rattled by and the planes roared overhead. When it was international war they pleaded their conscience; when it was class war, they fixed their bayonets.

> One fact of public interest for pacifist sympathizers with the Soviet regime is the position of the military here. They are far the most favored sector of the population: numerous, full of swagger, very much in evidence everywhere. Their boots, their overcoats, their bellies, the complexion—all mark them out in the streets as a privileged class.[4]

In a similar vein, visiting clergymen had a habit of hanging around anti-God museums.

In other writings, Muggeridge describes the joyless pall that hung over the populace: the fears, the privations, the cruelties large and small; the arrogance of the ruling classes, pictures of Stalin everywhere. He summed it all up in a diary entry.

> Sloan came to supper with us. We talked, of course, of Russia. He makes the Marxist case. I tried to explain to him why this place seemed so evil to me. Evil is the only apt word. Evil because there is no virture in it and because it has utterly failed. In a Marxist state, evil and failure are the same.[5]

The key notes emerging from Muggeridge's life at this stage are disillusionment and hopelessness. Kitty became ill; editors in England were cutting his articles to pieces. The Soviet authorities were not well disposed toward the man they once thought a disciple of Sidney Webb, whose *Theory and Practice of Trade Unionism* had been translated by none other than Lenin himself. Levity of any sort was indeed rare in those days. The dictatorship of the proletariat, as now, took itself seriously. Doubtless they reserved the jokes for the happy day when the state would fade away. Any comic relief would have to come from abroad because materialism in practice is unable to produce humor.

This turned out to be the case. The West that Muggeridge had fled rushed to his emotional rescue in the form of tours of foreign VIPs, clergy, and journalists.

I have never forgotten these visitors, or ceased to marvel at them, at how they have gone on from strength to strength, continuing to lighten our darkness, and to guide, counsel and instruct us; on occasion, momentarily abashed, but always ready to pick themselves up, put on their cardboard helmets, mount Rosinante, and go galloping off in yet another foray on behalf of the down-trodden and oppressed. They are unquestionably one of the wonders of the age, and I shall treasure till I die as a blessed memory the spectacle of them travelling with radiant optimism through a famished countryside, wandering in happy bands about squalid, overcrowded towns, listening with unshakeable faith to the fatuous patter of carefully trained and indoctrinated guides, repeating like schoolchildren a multiplication table, the bogus statistics and mindless slogans endlessly intoned to them. There, I would think, an earnest office-holder in some local branch of the League of Nations Union. There a godly Quaker who once had tea with Gandhi, there an inveigher against the Means Test and the Blasphemy Laws, there a staunch upholder of free speech and human rights, there an indomitable preventer of cruelty to animals; there scarred and worthy veterans of a hundred battles for truth, freedom and justice—all chanting the praises of Stalin and his dictatorship of the Proletariat. It was as though a vegetarian society had come out with a passionate plea for cannibalism, or Hitler had been nominated posthumously for the Nobel Peace Prize.[6]

Muggeridge and his colleagues diverted themselves by holding contests to see who could successfully pass off the most fatuous story to these visiting dignitaries. Malcolm managed to persuade Lord Marley that the long lines outside shops were part of the Soviet strategy to give the workers rest; otherwise the masses refused sleep in their zeal to build socialism. A.T. Cholerton overheard a British jurist ask a government official if the regime's legal system practiced habeas corpus. Cholerton interrupted, informing the fellow that he was not quite sure about habeas corpus but that the Russian authorities were strong on habeas cadaver.

While Shaw, Harold Laski, Lady Astor, the Huxleys, and their entourage spread tales of overflowing granaries and eager, well-fed workers, Malcolm managed to slip away to the Ukraine and examine the actual situation. His account is remarkably similar to that of Arthur Koestler. He saw people being loaded into trains like cattle and barely escaped being detained himself. At a railway stop he saw famished peasants fighting over scraps. When, back in England, Muggeridge described the horror of it, he was accused of being a liar and widely reviled. A famine in the Soviet Union? With its planned economy? Such a thing was unthinkable, impossible.

Muggeridge left the USSR via Riga, the capital of a then-independent Latvia. When they safely passed the border, people on the train began to spontaneously shout and shake their fists at the Soviet sentries. Observing the heavy fortifications, Muggeridge reflected that it was strange that a regime that needed to pen up its inhabitants behind barbed wire should still be able to make itself attractive to outsiders. But for him the attraction was gone forever.

The account of the lavish buffet at Riga station is also similar to Koestler's. After living in the USSR, the abundance came as a shock. Koestler found delight in observing people who were *individuals*, but Muggeridge, retreating as he was from Paradise and, like Adam and Eve, barred from reentry by a flaming sword, found it abhorrent.

Taking a strong dislike not only to the great dictatorship of the proletariat but also to its imbecilic (his word) foreign admirers was, he discovered, no laughing matter, whatever diversions the visitors had provided. Muggeridge launched a preemptive strike in the *English Review* entitled *"To The Friends of the Soviet Union."*

> That is to say, the dictatorship of the proletariat is cruel and arrogant; scornful of truth and liberty; indifferent to the suffering of individuals and classes and communities; incompetent and megalomaniac; ruthlessly intolerant of personal and corporate loyalties; hypocritical and stupid and corrupt, and has reduced a large population to a condition of poverty and misery and hopelessness that has to be seen to be believed. Nonetheless, dear Friends of the Soviet Union, you sniff round the dictatorship of the proletariat with craven adulation like dogs around ordure.[7]

His anxieties and difficulties drew him to George Orwell, who experienced the same sort of treatment for exposing the hypocrisy of communist policy in Spain.

> When I got to know him, we often discussed how difficult it is, in an ideologically polarized society like ours, to take up any position without being automatically assumed to hold all the views and attitudes associated with it. Like voting the ticket in an American election, when by just pressing one button support is automatically accorded to a whole string of candidates for all sorts of offices. Thus to attack the Soviet or the Spanish Republican regime was automatically to support their Fascist or Nazi opponents; to expose the fatuities of the liberal mind, to commend the authoritarian one.[8]

In those days, praising the Soviet Union was lucrative; attacking it involved penury, as the sale figures show. The road to revolution was paved with best-sellers. It bears repeating as well that Orwell's *Animal Farm* had such difficulty finding a home because of its anti-Stalin stance. When Khrushchev later revealed that there had indeed been horrible famine and, well, a few people had been, as they say, *liquidated*, none of those who had called Muggeridge a liar came forth to apologize. They had long since mounted Rosinante and galloped to the newest front. But his confrontations with them were not finished. During Khrushchev's postwar visit to Britain, a left-wing member of Parliament challenged Muggeridge to debate his position. At Oxford Union, Muggeridge successfully carried the motion, "This House refuses to believe that there has been any change in Russian policy of world domination." The vote went 237 to 173 in his favor.

Since he has begun to endlessly talk and write about Christianity, Muggeridge is often requested to reveal a Damascus road experience. He usually replies that, for him, the journey has been more that of Bunyan's Pilgrim. But without doubt the experiences in the Soviet Union, where, based on what he had seen, everything he had hitherto hoped and believed had been shattered, had purged him forever of what he calls "earthly solutions." He saw the prime motivating force of the age not as Inevitable Progress, but the reverse—a monumental death wish that would ultimately lay everything to waste, making of what remained of civilization one enormous *Kristallnacht*. The Nazi forces had their part to play, but so did another group.

> So had the credulous armies of the just, listening open-mouthed to Intourist patter, or seeking reassurance from a boozy sandalled Wicksteed, Wise old Shaw, high-minded Barbusse, the venerable Webbs, Gide the pure in heart and Picasso the impure, down to poor little teachers, crazed clergymen and millionaires, drivelling dons and very special correspondents like Duranty, all resolved, come what might, to believe anything, however villainous, to approve anything, however obscurantist and brutally authoritarian, in order to be able to preserve intact the confident expectation that one of the most thorough-going, ruthless and bloody tyrannies ever to exist on earth could be relied on to champion human freedom, the brotherhood of man, and all the other good liberal causes to which they had dedicated their lives. All resolved, in other words, to abolish themselves and their world, the rest of us with it. Nor have I from that time ever had the faintest expectation that, in earthly terms, anything could be salvaged; that any earthly battle could be won, or earthly solution found. It has all just been sleep-walking to the end of the night.[9]

From this detached viewpoint, Muggeridge has been able to see where it is all going. The prognostications—some would say prophecies—he made about the dissolution of the British Empire, the Sino-Soviet split, the revival of underground literature in the Soviet Union, have been uncannily fulfilled.

As he expected, the spiritual descendents of Duranty, Strong et al have carried on valiantly, enjoying great successes in Vietnam and Latin America. People believe lies, Muggeridge insists, not because they are plausible but, ultimately, because they want to believe them.

Neither did Muggeridge incline toward conspiracy theories. Behind the events he witnessed stood not labyrinthine plots, but a new kind of tyranny—that of the General

Idea described by French critic and historian Hippolyte Taine.

> There is nothing more dangerous than a General Idea in narrow, empty minds. Being empty, they are incapable of questioning it; being narrow, before long it becomes an obsession. Thenceforth it takes complete control of them. They are no longer their own master, but, in the most literal sense, possessed. [10]

Karl Marx provided the General Idea; the dictatorship of the proletariat and its admirers provided the narrow minds. And all of us have been affected.

Why has Muggeridge been less seriously regarded than his contemporaries who, after all, were wrong about the USSR?

In the West, particularly the Reformation countries, a long diet of sermons has caused wisdom to be associated with solemnity. Here Muggeridge has broken the rules. His writing has been satirical, iconoclastic, and barbed. Worst of all, he has dared to *laugh* at the fellow-traveling elite who must, at least until utopia dawns, take themselves with deadly seriousness. He has compared the World Council of Churches to a convention of drunkards holding on to each other lest, alone, they fall into the gutter. [11] Interviewing trendy clergymen on television, he would ask, "Bishop, is there an afterlife?" instead of inquiring about the Christian ethics of Third World communist guerrillas. He has continued to insist that Jesus' kingdom is not of this world, that carnal pursuits are vain and lead to misery, that abortion is *wrong*. These are among the most unpopular words it is possible to utter. From the point of view of the liberal-left media, it is blasphemy.

Muggeridge has also dared to suggest a reason for the adulation of totalitarianism. It is worthy of quotation in full and applicable to the dictatorship of the proletariat in many countries.

The answer, I believe, is terribly simple. A ghastly, fearful answer. You are indulgent towards the dictatorship of the proletariat because, in a sort of way, you are, or would like to be, a dictatorship of the proletariat yourselves. You are frustrated revolutionaries, and the spectacle of a revolutionary government in actual existence so intoxicates you that you fall on your knees, senses swooning, in awed worship. Like plain and reluctantly virtuous women fawning on brazen promiscuity you fawn on the dictatorship of the proletariat. When you hear of comrade so and so being taken for a ride you unconsciously lick your lips over the prospect of taking councillor so and so, who opposes your scheme for giving free milk to elementary school children, for a ride. The dictatorship of the proletariat is all-powerful and mouths your aspirations; and you, who have for so long had to be content with spinning your ideas into words, see in it the possibility of translating them into deeds. Seeing this, you adore; and adoring, you easily become propaganda-fodder.[12]

This undoubtedly correct analysis is, from the worshipful Marxist standpoint, even worse than ridicule. One can see some dour liberation theologian on a talk show frown, wrinkle his brow, and pronounce the malediction—"simplistic," quickly adding that such and such a conservative politician in the United States believes the same thing, so how can we take this seriously? With adulation of Marxist dictatorships a prevailing orthodoxy in much of the West, what Muggeridge feared has come to pass.

No worse fate can befall a society, dear Friends of the Soviet Union, than to fall into your hands. A General Idea is the most terrible of all tyrants. Individual tyrants have their moods, and must at last die; it is inflexible and immortal. Individual tyrants only require a sense of personal supremacy, only destroy whoever and whatever challenges their personal supremacy; it destroys everything and everyone, is the essence of destruction—in towns, a darkness, a paralysis; in the country, a blight, sterility. Shouting monotonously its empty formula—a classless, socialist society—it attacks with methodical barbarity, not only men and classes and institutions, but the soul of a society. It tears a society up by the roots and leaves it dead. "If we go," Lenin said, "We shall slam the door on an empty house."[13]

The prognosis is undoubtedly pessimistic. Muggeridge allows for the possibility of a new Dark Age. The West, like all human civilizations, is not forever. But what of the East and the USSR? Has he had intimations of changes there? He notes with joy that the Soviet authorities have been unable to stamp out religion, but has he foreseen anything apocalyptic?

On his second day in Moscow, 17 September 1932, Muggeridge visited Lenin's tomb, waiting with the long lines of people and finally observing the embalmed, glass-encased saint himself. (During another visit, to his great surprise, a woman crossed herself.) He did not quite know what to make of it. That evening he took out his diary and wrote:

> What do the thousands upon thousands of Russians who wait, sometimes a considerable time, to see him, make of the spectacle, I wondered. Their faces, quite blank. give away nothing. Here, I thought, is the one successful, even convincing, piece of ceremonial devised in modern times. But I had a queer conviction that one day an enraged mob would tear him from his place and trample him under foot.[14]

Until such a thing happens—if indeed it ever does—Muggeridge, like countless others through the centuries, has taken refuge in the City of God. Unlike all cities of man, it is forever. In the novel *Winter in Moscow*, Muggeridge sounds a note of hope. Wraithby (a name Muggeridge uses in fiction for himself) ventures into a church service.

> He left her and turned into a church. A service was going on with quite a large congregation, mostly peasants. A melancholy, passionate service. Religion was a refuge from the Dictatorship of the Proletariat. Priests in vestments and with long hair were chanting prayers; little candle flames lighting the darkness, and incense rising. The voices of the priests were dim like echoes, and the congregation curiously quiet; curiously still. Wraithby found their stillness hopeful; even exhilarating. It suggested that even general ideas spent themselves at last and were nothing.[15]

CHAPTER 7, NOTES
  1. Malcolm Muggeridge, *Like It Was: The Diaries of Malcolm Muggeridge* (New York: Morrow, 1982), 14.
  2. Malcolm Muggeridge, *Chronicles of Wasted Time* (New York: Morrow, 1973), 1:256.
  3. Muggeridge, *Like It Was*, 41.
  4. Ibid., 37.
  5. Ibid., 48.
  6. Muggeridge, *Wasted Time*, 1:244-45.
  7. Malcolm Muggeridge, *Things Past*, ed. Ian Hunter (New York: Morrow, 1978), 27.
  8. Muggeridge, *Wasted Time*, 1:273.
  9. Ibid., 1:275.
 10. Muggeridge, *Things Past*, 33.
 11. Malcolm Muggeridge, *Jesus Rediscovered* (London: Collins, 1969), 148.
 12. Muggeridge, *Things Past*, 31.
 13. Ibid., 33.
 14. Muggeridge, *Like It Was*, 15.
 15. Muggeridge, *Things Past*, 45.

CHAPTER 8
ARTHUR KOESTLER

I went to Communism as one goes to a spring of fresh water.
Pablo Picasso

I went to Communism as one goes to a spring of fresh water,
and I left Communism as one clambers out of a poisoned
river strewn with the wreckage of flooded cities and the
corpses of the drowned.   Arthur Koestler, *Invisible Writing*

In life and in letters, Arthur Koestler was something
of a decathlete.

He was, among other things, a member of a duelling
fraternity at the University of Vienna, a Zionist worker in a
Galilean kibbutz, lemonade vendor in Haifa, foreign correspondent, science editor, professional communist, prisoner
of war, and a member of a zeppelin expedition to the North
Pole.

Though best known for the novel *Darkness at Noon,* he
wrote many books including the novels *Arrival and Depar-
ture, The Gladiators* and *Thieves In The Night.* His autobio-
graphical works include *Dialogue With Death,* written as a result of his imprisonment by Franco, and *The Invisible Writing,*
which covers his activities as a communist, as did his seg-
ment of *The God That Failed.* Later writings included history,
The Thirteenth Tribe, and parapsychology, *The Roots of Coin-
cidence,* in addition to essays on many themes and the play
Twilight Bar. His writings were sometimes controversial,

sometimes attacked, but always elegant and never boring. Koestler considered it a distinction that, during his lifetime, both Hitler and Stalin designated his works for the flames.

He was born in Budapest in 1905, a time, he later wrote, when the sun was setting on the age of reason. In fact prodigies ran in the family, and he was no exception, though he claimed to acquire cleverness more rapidly than wisdom, something a reading of his autobiographies bears out.

Mathematics, science, and the construction of mechanical toys all interested the young Arthur. Before he finished his teens, he had attained fluency in Hungarian, German, French, and English. Chess was his main hobby. He was a short boy, which led to an inferiority complex described by a friend as being of cathedral proportions. During his childhood he was repeatedly subjected to bizarre punishments for even minor breaches of etiquette. This surely contributed to his lifelong sense of indignation with the established order.

Darwin, Spencer, Kepler, Marconi—these were his heroes. Ernst Haeckel's *Die Weltraetsel,* which purported to solve the seven riddles of the universe, served as a kind of sacred text. But there remained doubts in Koestler's mind regarding questions of infinity and eternity. As a child he pictured an arrow being shot into the blue and traveling on forever.[1] Spatial infinity was a mystery, a riddle that tortured his mind.

Koestler considered that perhaps he had been chosen to solve this riddle. He had a thirst for the absolute, but his search proved sterile. Some would say that he looked in the wrong places. In any case, his own arrow in the blue, unable to overcome the prevailing gravitational pull, plunged resolutely back to earth.

> The Infinite as a target was replaced by Utopias of one kind or another. It was the same quest and the same all-or-nothing mentality which drove me to the Promised Land and into the Communist Party. In other ages aspirations of this kind found their natural fulfillment in God. Since the

end of the eighteenth century, the place of God has been
vacant in our civilization; but during the ensuing century
and a half so many exciting things were happening that
people were not aware of it.[2]

Though Koestler possessed an exceptionally sharp
mind, he admitted that his political awakening came not
through cogent arguments aimed at the intellect but through
the emotions.

Just before the ascension to power of Béla Kun's communist dictatorship in Hungary, 1919, some members of the
Communist party were killed in a demonstration.
Thousands of workers joined the funeral procession that followed some days later. A band played Chopin's "Marche
Funebre." The event made a lasting impression on Koestler,
who was soon singing along with the Hungarian version of
the "Internationale," a verse of which ran:

To wipe out the past forever,
O army of slaves, follow us.
We shall lift the globe from its axis,
we are nothing, we shall be all.[3]

Koestler did not then take the plunge into the Communist party. He saw the differences on the left between the
liberals (German Democratic Party), the socialists, and the
communists as being of degree but not in kind. He and his
colleagues had no doubt that they were on the side of the
angels.

We were fervently anti-war, anti-militaristic, anti-
reactionary. . . . We believed in national self-determination, and freedom for the colonial people.[4]

Koestler signals three factors facilitating his enlistment
in what he called the SSS—Silent Soviet Services: idealism,
naivete, and the unscrupulousness of the voluntary helpers.

I was one of those half-virgins of the Revolution who
could be had by the SSS, body and soul, for the asking. I
mention this, not out of confessional urge, but because, as a
young man of average Central European background,

> endowed with the average amount of idealism and more than
> average experience, I consider my case as fairly typical. The
> Comintern and OGPU carried on a white-slave traffic whose
> victims were young idealists flirting with violence.[5]

After undergoing a gradual de-bourgeoisification involving the loss of jobs and the burning of ideological
bridges, Koestler finally joined the Communist party on the
last day of 1931. During the elections of 1931-32, he can-
vassed door to door, an activity he described as selling world
revolution like vacuum cleaners. For this duty, it was necessary to learn a new language in addition to the ones he had
already mastered.

Koestler sometimes refers to Stalin by his real,
Georgian last name, Dzhugashvili (or Djugashvili). The acceptable political dialect he dubbed "Djugashvilese."

> We cast off our intellectual baggage like passengers on a
> ship seized by panic, until it became reduced to the strictly
> necessary minimum of stock-phrases, dialectical clichés and
> Marxist quotations, which constitute the international jar-
> gon of Djugashvilese. To have shared the doubtful privilege
> of a bourgeois education, to be able to see several aspects of a
> problem and not only one, became a permanent cause of self-
> reproach. We craved to become single—and simple—
> minded. Intellectual self-castration was a small price to pay
> for achieving some likeness to Comrade Ivan Ivanovich.[6]

Thus Koestler willingly lobotomized himself for the
purpose of becoming as proletarian as possible. Intellectuals,
he later discovered, were a species to be tolerated and used,
just as the Nazis in their extermination camps marked certain skilled Jews with special armbands so that someone
would not mistakenly heave them into an oven before their
time. Koestler, as an intellectual, was to prove useful.

The reason for his dismissal from the Ullstein chain of
newspapers was not publicly known. He soon discovered
that one who had been fired for being a communist agent
could still work on a freelance basis for the same paper. It was
eventually decided that he should go to Russia masquerading

as a bourgeois journalist and write a series of articles on the first Five-Year Plan entitled, "The Soviet Land Through Bourgeois Eyes." The plan was to portray him as a bourgeois reporter who is initially antagonistic to the Soviet Union but sees the light through reporting on Soviet Reconstruction and eventually ends up a full and dutiful Comrade. Koestler already claimed to be "in love" with the Five-Year Plan. So much so, in fact, that he once considered writing a modern version of the Song of Songs dedicated to it:

> The eyes of my beloved shine like blast-furnaces in the steppe; her lips are boldly drawn like the White Sea Canal; her shoulder is slenderly curved like the Dnieper Dam; her spine is long and straight like the Turkestan-Siberian Railway . . . and the foxes, the little foxes that spoil the vine, were the counter-revolutionary fascist saboteurs.[7]

To facilitate Koestler's writing and conversion, he was wined and dined and extended special privilege beyond the wildest dreams of the average Russian. For a writer of his bent, it seemed like paradise, but he was later to discover some terrible truths.

When he arrived, much of the country experienced famine, a direct result of the forced collectivization of agriculture. But it was still possible to joke about conditions, even in the style of party propaganda:

> *Question:* What does it mean when there is food in the town but no food in the country?
>
> *Answer:* A Left, Trotskyite deviation.
>
> *Question:* What does it mean when there is food in the country but no food in the town?
>
> *Answer:* A Right, Bukharinite deviation.
>
> *Question:* What does it mean when there is no food in the country and no food in the town?
>
> *Answer:* The correct application of the general line.
>
> *Question:* What does it mean when there is food both in the country and in the town?
>
> *Answer:* The horrors of Capitalism.[8]

This anecdote, it is safe to say, tells more about the problem of food and hunger in socialist lands than many a turgid tome by Marxist economists. Not long after, however, when Stalin got into full stride as the master-terrorist of the age, there was nothing to laugh about.

> I saw the ravages of the famine of 1932-33 in the Ukraine: hordes of families in rags begging at the railway stations, the women lifting up to the compartment window their starving brats which—with drumstick limbs, big cadaverous heads, puffed bellies—looked like embryos out of alcohol bottles; the old men with frost-bitten toes sticking out of torn slippers. I was told that these were kulaks who had resisted the collectivization of the land and I accepted the explanation; they were enemies of the people who preferred begging to work.

If one cares to check the statements of Western luminaries and the reports in the Western press at the time, the picture is quite different. Not only was it adamantly denied that any such famine existed, but, furthermore, it was contended such a thing could never happen in a carefully planned economy such as that of the USSR.

As Koestler further describes in *The Invisible Writing* and *The God That Failed,* there were many other such shocks, though the shock absorbers of Koestler's dialectical training in double-think smoothed things out for a time. He left Russia in 1933. Back in Europe, he recalls being "blissfully happy," especially at the difference in the people.

> What struck me the most, the people in the train all had different personalities instead of being molecules in a grey, amorphous mass. They were mysteriously alive, they were individuals. [10]

Koestler might have ended his association with communism right then but for two things: the fight against the Nazis and the Spanish Civil War. He stayed in the party until 1938, an attachment he compares to drug addiction.

But the real show, applicable in many places today, was socialism versus the people. The purges and trials—part of the program—were on in earnest. When the blood began to flow and the victims to pile up, the elasticity of Koestler's mind reached its limit and snapped.

> Every one of us knows of at least one friend who perished in the Arctic subcontinent of forced labor camps, was shot as a spy or vanished without trace. How our voices boomed with righteous indignation, denouncing the flaws in the procedure of justice in our comfortable democracies; and how silent we were when our comrades, without trial or conviction, were liquidated in the Socialist sixth of the earth. Each of us carries a skeleton in the cupboard of his conscience; added together they would form galleries of bones more labyrinthine than the Paris catacombs.[11]

Koestler's arrow in the blue had not only returned to earth and landed in a fraudulent utopia, but it had struck him square in the heart. He resigned from the party, denounced the abuses, but still stubbornly clung to the illusion that the Soviet Union represented the last hope on a planet in rapid decay. Like Jacob, he had labored long and hard; he entered the dark tent, finding the next day that he had slept with an illusion, and a cruel one at that. But such were his ardors that he worked on. He explains why:

> I have only mentioned this epilogue to my Party days, my clinging to the last shred of the torn illusion, because it was typical of that intellectual cowardice which still prevails on the Left. The addiction to the Soviet myth is as tenacious as any other addiction. After the Lost Weekend in Utopia the temptation is strong to have just one last drop, even if watered down and sold under a different label. And there is always a supply of new labels on the Cominform's black market in ideals. They deal in slogans as bootleggers deal in faked spirits; and the more innocent the customer, the more easily he becomes a victim of the ideological hooch sold under the trade-mark of Peace, Democracy, Progress or what you will.[12]

For Koestler the final, clean break only came with the Hitler-Stalin pact of 23 August 1939, when the swastika was hoisted in Moscow alongside the hammer and sickle. (The symbols do resemble each other.) He pulled out the arrow but felt the wound the rest of his life:

> Those who were caught by the great illusion of our time, and have lived through its moral and intellectual debauch, either give themselves up to a new addiction of the opposite type, or are condemned to pay with a lifelong hangover. "They are the ambulant cemeteries of their murdered friends; they carry their shrouds as their banner."[13]

But do the many and varied experiences of one of the most versatile men of letters of our age belong only to history? Or does any of it apply today? It is fitting that Koestler should have the last word.

> As I am writing this, more than twenty years later, the storm is still on. The well-meaning "progressives of the Left" persist in following their old, outworn concepts. As if under the spell of a destructive compulsion, they must repeat every single error of the past, draw the same faulty conclusions a second time, re-live the same situations, perform the same suicidal gestures. One can only watch in horror and despair, for this time, there will be no pardon.[14]

Perhaps this horror and despair of witnessing the repetition of his own errors got to him. He died in March 1983, in a suicide pact with his third wife.

CHAPTER 8, NOTES
1. Arthur Koestler, *Arrow in the Blue* (New York; Macmillan, 1952), 51.
2. Ibid., 51-52.
3. Ibid., 64.
4. Ibid., 234-35.
5. Arthur Koestler, in *The God That Failed*, ed. Richard Crossman (New York: Harper, 1949), 37.
6. Ibid., 49.
7. Koestler, *Arrow in the Blue*, 287.
8. Koestler, *Invisible Writing*, 72.
9. Koestler in *The God That Failed*, 60.
10. Koestler, *Invisible Writing*, 199.
11. Koestler, *The God That Failed*, 71.
12. Ibid., 74.
13. Ibid., 55-56.
14. Koestler, *Arrow in the Blue*, 235-36.

CHAPTER 9
ANDRÉ GIDE

When asked at age eighty what he had most enjoyed, André Gide replied, "The *Arabian Nights*, the Bible, the pleasures of the flesh, and the kingdom of God."[1]

This just about summed him up. His life was a long conflict between the perennial duelists of carnality and holiness, with the former enjoying a distinct advantage. Malcolm Muggeridge likened his company to being in a cathedral when all the drains were plugged. Gide proclaimed himself a man in whom all contradictions were allowed free play.

André Gide—scarcely remembered in America—was once considered Europe's greatest living writer. He enjoyed a certain notoriety; his books once occupied a place on the Vatican's Index of Forbidden Literature and were later banned by the communists as well. In spite of this, he received the Nobel Prize for literature in 1947. He died in 1951.

He was born in Paris in 1869 to parents of Huguenot lineage. They gave him a strict religious upbringing, educating him privately and at the *École Alsacienne* in Paris. In France, this association with Protestantism undoubtedly provided a sense of being part of a minority. Gide's works include his *Journal, The Vatican Swindle, The Counterfeiters*,

The Pastoral Symphony, and two books on the Soviet Union, one highly adulatory, the other just as strong in condemnation.

That Gide should be attracted to a Worker's Paradise is not surprising. He inherited a large fortune and never endured a day of physical labor in his life. In addition he was French, and France was the power most derided in the period between the wars, much as the United States is today. In Gide, one can see the forces of guilt at work.

Thinking himself tubercular, Gide traveled to Africa in the midtwenties. He found the exploitation of the natives by their white masters shocking and pleaded their cause in two travel books *Voyage au Congo* and *Le Retour du Tchad. Voyage Au Congo,* dedicated to Conrad, was much praised by two other important writers of the French Left, Louis Aragon and André Malraux. The perception that the Soviet Union also championed the downtrodden and oppressed led him to declare that he had always been a communist at heart, even when he had been most Christian. In the USSR, he wrote in his *Journal,* they had abolished the decree, "Thou shalt earn *my* bread by the sweat of *thy* brow."[2]

> Why do I long for Communism? Because I believe it to be equitable and because I suffer on account of the injustices which I feel more strongly than ever when it is I myself who am favored. Because the regime under which we live does not seem to me to protect men from the most grievous abuses. Because among conservatives I see only dead or dying things. Because it seems to be absurd to cling to things that have had their day.[3]

Thus it was not Marx that brought Gide to communism. Indeed, Gide said that he had made strenuous efforts to read Marx—all in vain. He claimed brotherhood with those who had attained communism "through love." Though he once stated that if called upon to give his life for the Soviet Union he would gladly do so, he never joined any Communist party.

Other ex-fellow travelers (a Soviet locution) speak of

their personal *Kronstadt,* the event that turned them against the USSR once and for all. The reference is to the rebellion of sailors on the Island of Kronstadt near Petrograd. They demanded free speech, a secret ballot, and other bourgeois trifles and were brutally put down by the Bolsheviks, thus hardening opposition to the regime. The Nazi-Soviet pact was the *Kronstadt* for Fischer and Koestler, but not for Gide. At the behest of the Soviet Society of Authors, Gide visited the Soviet Union in June 1936. This was all it took.

Gide spoke at Gorki's funeral. Russian officials put on a great show for him doubtless expecting reams of hosannas from his pen in years to come. But it was not to be. Gide was too perceptive not to see the gap between illusion and reality.

An inveterate antifascist, Gide noticed that certain slogans, such as BELIEVE! OBEY! FIGHT!, were equally at home on a wall in Mussolini's fascist Italy or Stalin's communist Russia. What was worse, everyone thought alike:

> In the Soviet Union it is accepted once and for all that on every subject—whatever may be the issue—there can only be one opinion, the right one. And each morning *Pravda* tells the people what they need to know, and must believe and think.[4]

This was unacceptable to an individualist like Gide. On the same subject, he adds:

> I doubt whether in any country in the world—not even in Hitler's Germany—have the mind and spirit ever been less free, more bent, more terrorized over—and indeed vassalized—than in the Soviet Union.[5]

Neither did he find that exploitation had ended:

> The disappearance of capitalism has not brought freedom to the Soviet workers—it is essential that the proletariat abroad should realize this fully. It is of course true that they are no longer exploited by shareholding capitalists, but nevertheless they are exploited, and in so devious, subtle and twisted a manner that they do not know any more whom to blame.[6]

With all his considerable literary powers, Gide goes on to describe the awful conditions, the fear, the informers everywhere, the ugly buildings, the shabby clothes, the privileges of a special class—the bureaucrats. His disillusionment was complete, bottomless, just as his praise had been nearly stratospheric.

On the question of the possibility of human reform, Gide came full circle, back to a position resembling the Christianity of his youth.

> There is no doubt that all the bourgeois vices and failings still lie dormant, in spite of the Revolution, in many. Man cannot be reformed from the outside—a change of heart is necessary.[7]

Had there been any real change at all in the Soviet Union? Gide's answer constitutes not only a devastating indictment, but a chilling prophecy as well:

> The same old capitalist society has been re-established, a new and terrible despotism crushing and exploiting man, with all the abject and servile mentality of serfdom. Russia, like Demophoön, has failed to become a God and she will never now arise from the fires of the Soviet ordeal.[8]

Gide was not alone in this prediction. Orwell thought the Soviet Union so repressive that all hope of liberty there was forever lost. It remains true that not only the USSR but no other nation subjected to the new serfdom has ever escaped. The apologists of these regimes doubtless consider this a good thing. What Gide wrote not so long ago remains true:

> My mistake, at first, was to believe all the praise I heard, and everything which might have enlightened me was always said in a spiteful tone of voice. It happens too often that the friends of the Soviet Union refuse to see anything bad there—or at least to recognize it—so it happens that the truth is spoken with hatred and falsehood with love.[9]

So it continues to this day.

CHAPTER 9, NOTES
1. *Twentieth Century Authors* (New York: Wilson, 1955), 362.
2. André Gide in *The God That Failed*, ed. Richard Crossman (New York: Harper, 1949), 166.
3. Ibid., 168.
4. Ibid., 182.
5. Ibid., 188.
6. Ibid., 183
7. Ibid.
8. Ibid., 195.
9. Ibid., 178.

CHAPTER 10
MILOVAN DJILAS

W hen *The New Class* by Milovan Djilas, a Yugoslavian, appeared in the fifties, the *New York Times* called it "one of the most compelling and perhaps the most important sociological document of our time." The book created an international storm. Yet in the current political debate, the author's name is seldom, if ever, mentioned.

The thesis of *The New Class* is that not only has the state failed to wither away and classes to disappear as promised, but the very opposite has happened: the rulers of communist countries are the most entrenched aristocracy in history. As Djilas put it:

> There is also a difference between Communists and absolute monarchy. The monarchy did not think quite as highly of itself as the Communists do of themselves, nor was it as absolute as they are. . . .
> In contrast to earlier revolutions, the Communist revolution, conducted in the name of doing away with classes, has resulted in the most complete authority of any single new class. Everything else is sham and illusion.[1]

One can picture these lines going off like IRA letter bombs in the minds of Tito and the members of his court. The best monitor of the accuracy of any book about totalitarianism is the reaction it provokes in the ruling elite. For the New Aristocracy, *The New Class* was too much, especially coming from one of their own, the vice-president of Yugoslavia. Djilas claims the book would not seem strange to someone from the communist world; the problem lay in its truth. A Soviet censor once told Malcolm Muggeridge that he could not publish a story "because it was true." This was very much the case with Djilas. They banned the book and tossed the author into jail.

But he had been there before.

Milovan Djilas was born in the then-independent kingdom of Montenegro, later to be incorporated into Yugoslavia. He was one of seven children. The year was 1911. At that time, Montenegro—in fact all the Balkan states—reeled from long-standing and bloody feuds. "It seemed to me," Djilas wrote, "that I was born with blood on my eyes. My first sight was of blood."[2]

At eighteen he entered the university of Belgrade, where he earned a law degree. He also gained respect as a poet and short story writer, and notoriety as a leader of leftist students. In *Memoir of a Revolutionary*, he describes the budding of rebellion:

> Youthful rebellion first assumed a moral form: the nega-
> tion of traditional views and relationships. The common
> man suffered the dictatorship and the other hardships as
> elementary evils which had rendered him helpless. His con-
> centration was on his family life. He was petit bourgeois. But
> he did not have any choice if he was not willing to go to
> prison. Opposition to this kind of life, resistance to it and the
> bourgeois existence, was the most frequent form rebellion
> took among young people, particularly among intellectuals.[3]

Djilas and his fellow students rejected the bourgeois God along with the ideals of a past age, even revolutions of the past.

> We quickly distinguished ourselves from our predecessors:
> we felt that Marxism, as a discipline, could explain every-
> thing. Earlier revolutionaries possessed no such "complete"
> or "all-knowing" ideology, but, rather, a mixture of ideas

such as nationalism, Eastern Orthodoxy, and so on. We had only one idea, one ideology. Any remnant of "old" worn-out ideas was a weakness.[4]

In those days, Marxism indeed seemed an idea whose time had come. The students in Belgrade and other European cities had every reason to consider it the wave of the future.

> Communism and Communists were being discussed; Communist literature, predominantly in the form of fiction, was being published. The atmosphere was ripe for Communism. Communists favored a revolution, the overthrow of the existing system; they alone were being tortured in jails, and murdered. They were the only group that posed a real threat to the dictatorship.[5]

Djilas joined the illegal Communist party in 1932 and was arrested for organizing demonstrations against the monarchy, contemptuously referred to by communists as "King Alexander the Last." He served a three year sentence in Sremska Mitrovica prison. The guards tortured him in a variety of ways: beating the bottom of his feet, placing pencils between the toes and squeezing them, and wrenching his testicles while making jokes about, "castrating all communists." The treatment drove him to attempt suicide.

Before being thrown in jail, Djilas had fallen in love with a girl named Mitra Matrovic. She would stand outside the prison where he could see her. But although she knew his cell, she could see only his hands. Djilas reports that she did not miss a single Saturday. His descriptions of her and their relationship are truly touching. Unlike others, his involvement in revolutionary activity had not bilked him of humanity.

Prison officials stopped the torture and placed Djilas in solitary confinement, ostensibly hoping that he would think over his sins and repent. But his revolutionary ardor remained strong.

> But I, and this goes for most of my Communist friends, experienced no repentance, no longing for the past life, except

as a physical desire for good food, the countryside, and friends. I spent my time in jail concocting the most fantistic revolutionary schemes and adventures.[6]

If Djilas repented of anything, it was of sins against the party. His description of this process shows how guilt stricken the Marxist mindset is.

> Throughout my life as a Communist, I always felt a sense of guilt toward the party for one reason or another. No sooner would I forget one "sin" than I would come up with another. Every Communist I knew had the same experience—that goes for even the highest-ranking functionaries, absolutely without exception. They felt guilty because of some political slip-up, some ideological activity, a secret passion for women, or failure at police interrogation. I might even go so far as to say the better the Communist the more intense feelings of guilt. This phenomenon can be explained in terms of the party's dogmatic and sectarian character. But there was one more thing: the constant conflict between one's instincts and the nature of Communism, which seeks to subjugate man completely.[7]

One gets the feeling that, at that point, Djilas stood among those completely subjugated.

A revolutionary named Caki had taken part in an assassination attempt on King Alexander. Prison officials moved him in with Djilas. Djilas's observations on this man provide an interesting early picture of a Christian radical, especially in view of the increasing number of "liberation theologians" as they are known today.

> He was a strange mixture of religion and revolutionary struggle. He urged us to believe in God and he preached the justice and equality of the Bible: love all men, even those who hate you; conquer everything and everybody with love, or, still better, win over with goodness. But when he spoke of his former life, he would forget about God and his Biblical truth, and he'd sound like a revolutionary in old-fashioned language and thinking, but hard and adamant toward the enemy of his class.[8]

But Caki's God, along with his Scriptures, gave way to new deities and new texts. Quotes from Marx, Engels, and

Stalin were considered inerrant and sufficed to end the most complicated arguments. Djilas spurned heaven for paradise in this world, to be brought in within two or three generations. All the evidence seemed to point in that direction. He believed in the vision.

The elections of 1935 brought in a new administration more favorable to the revolutionaries. When released in 1937, Djilas met Josip Broz (Tito), general secretary of the Yugoslav Communist party. Together they helped to organize an international brigade to fight Franco in Spain. Djilas had passed out of his idealist phase and into the ranks of the working professionals. This did not mean that his ideological beliefs wavered. On the contrary, his reaction to the Nazi-Soviet pact shows that they solidified.

> I actually approved of the Soviet-German pact, as did most of the leading Communists, with only a few minor misgivings. We had already trained ourselves to have absolute confidence in the Soviet Union and in the decisions of its government. But there was another, more profound, reason. Theoretically speaking, we Communists had not ruled out collaboration between the Soviet Union and capitalist countries. All the capitalist countries were more or less the same for us. We saw no fundamental difference between Hitler's Germany and the Western democracies. It was simply a question of how useful a certain country could be to us at a certain moment in history.[9]

Thus an event that shattered the faith of Koestler, Fischer, and countless others was viewed by Djilas in simply utilitarian terms. Djilas reports violently attacking anyone with the slightest reservations about collaboration with the Nazis.

In 1940, Djilas became part of the party's politburo. When the useful Nazis finally occupied the Balkans, Djilas fought heroically with the partisan resistance. His father, two brothers, and two sisters were killed.

His wartime meetings with Stalin, described in the book *Conversations With Stalin*, got him in trouble with the Great Leader. He criticized the behavior of Red Army troops in Yugoslavia, citing the number of rapes for which they were responsible. It was the beginning of a rift with Moscow. In the Yugoslav postwar government, Djilas became minister of agitation and propaganda. Yugoslavia broke with the USSR in 1948.

Djilas rose to the vice-presidency in 1953, but even in this lofty post he got into trouble. He made the mistake of urging democratization and the relaxation of repression. In addition, he attacked the snobbery of the party officials and their wives. To paraphrase *Animal Farm,* Djilas looked from the revolutionaries back to the monarchists and from the monarchists to the revolutionaries, and could not tell the difference. Tito, Djilas's faithful comrade, charged him with the awful crime of being "influenced by the West," where the twin perils of democratization and moderation were rife.

In 1954 Djilas turned in his party card and began giving interviews to the foreign press. When the Hungarians revolted against the Soviets in 1956, Djilas praised and supported their revolution in a *New York Leader* article. This got him arrested for "hostile propaganda." They sentenced him to a three year term in, of all places, Sremska Mitrovica prison. It is rumored that he occupied the same cell as in his earlier stretch under the previous monarchy. Marxists are among history's most efficient jailers.

The New Class appeared in 1957, one of the few genuine literary events in history, a true blockbuster. But actual members of the new class were not amused. Like good civil libertarians they held a series of secret trials and added seven years to Djilas's sentence. This probably served as a parable for Djilas's belief that the new aristocracy was more severe than the old. For good measure, they stripped their fellow revolutionary fighter and resistance hero of all his decorations. To these indignities he responded.

> The heroic era of Communism is past. The epoch of its great leaders has ended. The epoch of practical men has set in. The new class has been created. It is at the height of its power and wealth, but it is without new ideas. It has nothing

more to tell the people. The only thing that remains is for it to justify itself.[10]

This justification did not, indeed cannot, occur in a vacuum.

> Having achieved industrialization, the new class can now do nothing more than strengthen its brute force and pillage the people. It ceases to create. Its spiritual heritage is overtaken by darkness.[11]

As Lenin so succinctly put it—who whom? That is the question; who does what to whom. It is inescapable; in a planned society, there are the planners and the planned. Or, as the Great Helmsman Mao's version has it: power comes from the barrel of a gun. In a socialist state, there abideth illusion, propaganda, and power, but the greatest of these is power. Djilas sees this most clearly:

> Communist regimes are a form of latent civil war between the government and the people.[12]

When one considers the man-made famines, the forced labor, the purges, the fraudulent trials, it becomes clear that this constant civil war is more than latent. It is a permanent *jihad*. The new class must wage this holy war because, according to the theory, they are infallible and must be seen as such.

All through *The New Class* there run strata of eloquence, rage, incisive analysis, and the odd felicitous putdown. For instance, Djilas calls communist parliaments, "mausoleums." To the notion that communism is a transition to something else, he snaps, "This leads nowhere and explains nothing. What is not a transition to something else?"[13] But a complete impression of *The New Class* can only be gained by a careful reading of the entire text. However, some of his observations must be quoted.

In Djilas's day, as now, admirers and defenders of totalitarian countries include pacifists and practitioners of nonviolence. Yet, what these people most abominate—

militarism—not only thrives best under the auspices of the new class, but is inherent in its system.

> Founded by force and violence, in constant conflict with its people, the Communist state, even if there are no external reasons, must be militaristic. The cult of force, especially military force, is nowhere so prevalent as in Communist countries. Militarism is the internal basic need of the new class; it is one of the forces which make possible the new class's existence, strength and privileges.[14]

As British writer Os Guinness has explained, for a long time it has been assumed that to be on the left is to be intelligent, as opposed to allegedly unthinking reactionaries on the right. In the ranks of fellow travelers, intellectuals have been numerous. But according to Djilas, the new class is leading the way to the abolition of intelligence.

> The intellectual inheritance of the people is also being confiscated. The monopolists act as if all history has occurred just to let them make their appearance in the world. They measure the past and everything in it by their own likeness and form, and apply a single measure dividing all men and phenomena into "progressive" and "reactionary" classification. In this fashion they raise up monuments. They elevate the pygmies and destroy the great, especially the great of their own time.
>   Their "single scientific" method is most suitable too in that it alone protects and justifies their exclusive dominance over science and society.[15]

And what of art? Does this precious gift, the very occupation of so many fellow travelers, flourish under the new class? Tito thought textbooks more valuable than novels.[16] In the USSR, all forms of artistic expression were forbidden except those that Stalin himself liked, and the man was not a bastion of good taste. The Soviet Union continues to churn out turgid novels on "girl meets tractor" themes. The artist as a freethinker—an independent, creative entity—is anathema to the new class for obvious reasons.

> A work of art, by its very nature, is usually a criticism of a given situation and of given relations. In Communist systems, therefore, artistic creation based on actual subjects is

not possible. Only praise of a given situation or criticism of
the system's opponents is permitted. Under those terms art
can have no value whatever.[17]

Who could argue against championing the down-
trodden and oppressed? Who could be against peace and the
brotherhood of man? Not this writer. Not anyone with more
than an atom of humanity, and certainly not Djilas. But the
question is whether the new class has any claim to the admi-
rations of those who pursue these worthy aims:

> Honor, sincerity, sacrifice, and love of the truth were
> once things that could be understood for their own sakes:
> now, deliberate lies, sycophancy, slander, deception, and
> provocation gradually become the inevitable attendants of
> the dark, intolerant, and all-inclusive might of the new
> class, and even affect relations between the members of the
> class.[18]

We are often reminded of Soviet gallantry in the Second World War, and how they lost some twenty million
men. The assumption is that these souls sacrificed themselves for the new and happy life under the aegis of socialism.
Djilas disagrees:

> Communist totalitarianism leads to total discontent, in
> which all differences of opinion are gradually lost, except
> despair and hatred. Spontaneous resistance—the dissatisfac-
> tion of millions with the everyday details of life—is the form
> of resistance that the Communists have not been able to
> smother. This was confirmed during the Soviet-German
> war. When the Germans first attacked the USSR, there
> seemed to be little desire for resistance among the Russians.
> However, Hitler soon revealed that his intentions were the
> destruction of the Russian state and the changing of the
> Slavs and other Soviet peoples into impersonal slaves of the
> Herrenvolk. From the depths of the people there emerged the
> traditional, unquenchable love for the homeland. During
> the entire war Stalin did not mention either the Soviet gov-
> ernment or its socialism to the people; he mentioned only
> one thing—the homeland. And it was worth dying for, in
> spite of Stalin's socialism.[19]

Thus Stalin promoted what his admirers despised—
patriotism, the traditional love of country. What Djilas does

not mention is that Stalin also whistled to a far corner of the gulag for the metropolitan of the Russian Orthodox church and put him to work on three shifts reviving the myths of Holy Russia, a kind of Eastern God 'n' country combination.

Djilas regarded Stalin, whom he knew personally, as the greatest criminal in history:

> Every crime was possible to Stalin, for there was not one he had not committed. Whatever standards we use to take his measure, in any event—let us hope for all time to come— to him will fall the glory of being the greatest criminal in history. For in him was joined the criminal senselessness of a Caligula with the refinement of a Borgia and the brutality of a Tsar Ivan the Terrible.[20]

Many would agree, even some members of the current Soviet new class. But Stalin is gone, it is argued, even as a piece of interesting taxidermy beside Lenin. One further hears the contention that the master criminal who ruled the USSR for thirty years was an aberration, the exception, not the rule. But the question remains, Have things changed since his death? Djilas doesn't think so.

> Today it is fashionable, and to some extent justifiable, to evaluate Soviet policy as it was before and after Stalin's death. However, Stalin did not invent the systems, nor do those who succeeded him believe in them less than he did. What has changed since his death is the method by which Soviet leaders handle relations between systems, not the systems themselves.[21]

Elsewhere, Djilas acknowledges that some systems have indeed changed.

> The breakdown of Western capitalism through crises and wars did not take place. In 1949 Vishinsky, at the United Nations, in the name of the Soviet leadership, predicted the beginning of a great new crisis in the United States and in capitalism. The opposite happened. This was not because capitalism is good or bad, but because the capitalism the Soviet leaders rant about no longer exists.[22]

But the new class still exists and has quite a recruitment drive going, proclaiming slavery to the free and darkness to those in light. Does Djilas have any counsel for those who would live independently of them?

> Unfortunately, even now, after the so-called De-Stalinization, the same conclusion can be reached as before: Those who wish to live and to survive in a world different from the one Stalin created and which in essence and in full force still exists must fight.[23]

This call to action is perhaps part of the reason Djilas is seldom mentioned, especially in liberal circles. If only he had advocated summit meetings, cultural exchanges, earnest negotiations, or concessions, or disarmament, or pacifism. Then he might have been popular.

CHAPTER 10, NOTES
1. Milovan Djilas, *The New Class* (New York: Praeger, 1957), 3, 36.
2. *Current Biography* (New York: Wilson, 1943), 119.
3. Milovan Djilas, *Memoir of a Revolutionary* (New York: Harcourt, Brace, Jovanovich, 1973), 9.
4. Ibid., 95.
5. Ibid., 97.
6. Ibid., 159.
7. Ibid., 165.
8. Ibid., 203-4.
9. Ibid., 329.
10. Djilas, *The New Class*, 53-54.
11. Ibid., 69.
12. Ibid., 87.
13. Ibid., 172.
14. Ibid., 95.
15. Ibid., 136.
16. Ibid., 138.
17. Ibid., 139.
18. Ibid., 156.
19. Ibid., 99.
20. Milovan Djilas, *Conversations With Stalin* (New York: Harcourt Brace Jovanovich, 1963), 187.
21. Djilas, *The New Class*, 197.
22. Ibid., 212.
23. Djilas, *Conversations With Stalin*, 191.

CHAPTER 11
GEORGE ORWELL

Оne hesitates to write about George Orwell because, in recent years, the tide of Orwelliana on both sides of the Atlantic has been overwhelming.

In addition, Orwell's case is not quite the same as those of Fischer and Koestler. He never went to the USSR. His experiences in Marxist-controlled areas were limited to Spain during the civil war. Neither did he ever, as some claim, cease to be a socialist, even though the malevolent ideology of his novel 1984 was INGSOC—English socialism. Though the book was a powerful antitotalitarian tract, it did not mean that its author had deserted the left. Orwell continued to support the British Labour party.

In a recent *Harper's* article, Norman Podhoretz claimed that if Orwell were alive today, he would be a neoconservative. (A reader wrote ridiculing this idea, adding that Bella Abzug might just as easily contend that if Orwell were alive today, he would be a woman.) Orwell died in 1950—on Lenin's birthday. We can only speculate what his ideology might have been today. As it stands, he remained a socialist, something that saddened Canadian critic Barbara Amiel:

But, like Camus, Orwell's most scathing criticism was focused on what he considered to be the moral lapses of the socialist position—an annoying habit for socialists, whose doctrine centers on a belief of having cornered the market in morality. It was this attitude that repeatedly caused them to suggest that, in the end, Orwell had abandoned the fold.

But Orwell had not. His whole being, however, centered on such qualities as independence, clarity, inventiveness, honesty and spunk. For a man of these facets to select socialism—with its demands for drab, institutionalized thinking and blinkered adherence to dogma—as his political philosophy was a little bit like a ballet master getting work as a trainer of elephants.[1]

A social descender of sorts, Orwell was also solidly middle-class, an Etonian, who put in a stint with the Imperial Police in Burma before going native himself and crawling through the entrails of Paris and London (see *Down and Out in Paris and London*). Here he became attached to the working class and developed a socialist political creed.

Though a socialist, he was the very conscience of a movement at that time largely composed of political reprobates. "So much of left-wing thought," he wrote, "is a kind of playing with fire by people who don't even know that fire is hot."[2]

George Orwell knew that fire was hot; he was not above angry diatribes directed at political and intellectual faddists:

"... the astute young social literary climbers who are Communists now, as they will be Fascists five years hence because it is all the go, and all that dreary tribe of high-minded women and sandal-wearers and bearded fruit-juice drinkers who come flocking toward the smell of 'progress' like bluebottles to a dead cat."[3]

This is particularly applicable now that the best definition for communism, as Susan Sontag has pointed out, is successful fascism.

Reading Orwell's collection of essays, *Inside the Whale*, which includes "The Prevention of Literature" and "Politics and the English Language," one feels that it was written for today. He seems more at home with the essay form than the novel. Like his friend Muggeridge, Orwell loved words and resented their distortion by the apologists of totalitarian states. He exposed such doublespeak as *pacification* for "bombing" and *liquidation* for "murder." One example is worthy of quotation in full:

> Consider for instance some comfortable English professor defending Russian totalitarianism. He cannot say outright, "I believe in killing off your opponents when you can get good results by doing so." Probably, therefore, he will say something like this:
>
> "While freely conceding that the Soviet régime exhibits certain features which the humanitarian might be inclined to deplore, we must, I think, agree that a certain curtailment of the right to political opposition is an unavoidable concomitant of transitional periods, and that the rigors which the Russian people have been called upon to undergo have been amply justified in the sphere of concrete achievement."[4]

He goes on to point out that the real enemy of clear language is insincerity, a gap between one's real and one's declared aims. Then, as now, language had become a tool of distortion instead of elucidation. Examples of this inflated nonlanguage, expressing nonthoughts and nonhopes, abound in our time.

Orwell's polemics, in fact, are not only still studied but still occasionally make news. He once wrote criticizing Dr. Alex Comfort (author of *The Joy of Sex*) who had intimated that a Nazi takeover of England would not really be all that bad. The piece was alluded to in a December 1982 *Harper's* article called "Tidings of Comfort and Joy" and drew a letter of protest from Comfort himself. The author of "Tidings," J. P. Corkery, calmly defended himself by referring the readers to the original article and Orwell's response in his *Collected Journalism.*

A form of debate sometimes used by socialists and liberals is to call those who disagree with them "fascists." The term is sometimes shouted from the socialist New Democratic Party benches in Canadian provincial legislatures.

Joan Baez, describing a reluctant visit to Disneyland, said that she felt uncomfortable among "all the fascists." One wonders how she knew they were fascists. Did she poll them on their love for national socialism? Were they wearing Mussolini-style black shirts? Did she inquire as to their anti-Semitic prejudices? Hardly. To qualify for the label, one need only be a mainstream American and show up at Disneyland on the same day as Joan Baez.

Commenting on this sort of thing in 1947, Orwell said that so much ignorance surrounded the term "fascist" that its only remaining meaning was "something not desirable." Clearly, he was ahead of his time. In fact various socialists and more particularly communists accused Orwell of not only being a fascist himself ("objectively fascist" it was put) but of aiding the fascist cause in the Spanish war. What did Orwell do to deserve such abuse? First, some background on Spain.

In 1936, a coalition of leftist Republicans and Socialists narrowly won the Spanish national elections. The right viewed this marriage uneasily, especially when Socialist leader Largo Caballero spoke of easing the Republicans out and establishing a dictatorship of the proletariat. The *Falange,* founded by José Antonio Primo de Rivera, fought socialism and appealed to the military to save the country from Marxism. Francisco Franco, Emilio Mola, and Manuel Goded formed an officers' conspiracy. Their coup had been prepared for a long time. But the murder of right-wing monarchist Calvo Sotelo launched them into action. The right, known as the Nationalists, mutinied against the government, a reversal of most modern revolutions in which the antigovernment forces are leftist.

Franco had been sent to the Canary Islands to keep him out of politics. He landed in Morocco, mobilized forces, and crossed into Spain, taking Andalusia and other southern areas with little trouble. Catalonia and the Basque provinces remained loyal to the government because they had been promised autonomy.

Largo Caballero was ousted as leader and replaced by Juan Negrin. The Communist party grew in numbers and influence since they controlled the influx of arms from the Soviet Union.

Abroad, solidarity with the government was widespread. The rebel Nationalists, after all, sought to overthrow an elected government. International Brigades were organized; among them the Mackenzie-Papineau Brigade from Canada (known as the Mac-Paps) and the Abraham Lincoln Brigade from the United States. These, along with tanks, aircraft, and a military mission from the Soviet Union, soundly trounced Nationalist forces in several key battles and kept Franco from taking Madrid. *No pasarán*—they will not pass—became the battle cry.

Franco received ample supplies from Germany and Italy in the form of artillery and tanks and the one hundred-plane Condor Division that practically destroyed the Basque town of Guernica, 26 April 1937. Picasso commemorated the attack in a painting.

The Spanish civil war was cruel and deadly, with atrocities on both sides. Dissention between communists and anticommunists helped Franco to take Madrid and end the war. Britain recognized the Nationalists on 27 February 1939, France the next day, and the United States a month later.

The Nationalist regime constituted more of a restoration of feudalism than an establishment of fascism, as even Orwell pointed out. Though Franco's reign was oppressive and long, Spain has evolved since his death, with Felipe Gonzalez's Socialist party now in power by virtue of an election win. Spain is also the newest member of NATO, something that Franco might not have approved.

How eager was Orwell to fight Franco and fascism? He pawned the family silver to finance the trip, planning to both write and fight. But he found that unity on the government side did not exist. Orwell joined the *Partido Obrero de Unificación Marxista*, the POUM, an anarcho-syndicalist group with its own militia. The Soviet-backed communists regarded the POUM as "Trotskyite," and the group was vilified in the international press. *Pravda* announced on 16 December 1936, with its usual subtlety: "In Catalonia, the elimination of Trotskyites and Anarcho-Syndicalists has begun. It will be carried out with the same energy as it was carried out in the Soviet Union."[5] Tales spread that the POUM held direct ties with the fascists. Liberal newspapers in Britain picked up the stories; Orwell read them with disgust and anger. Communist officials in the Spanish government urged the "extermination" of groups such as the POUM. Terror prevailed. There were riots in Barcelona. More than a few innocent people were murdered.

Orwell fought valiantly against the Nationalists but one day caught a sniper's bullet in the neck. Had he been hit a millimeter to the left he would have been killed, but he recovered completely, with his voice only slightly affected. He returned to England to write it all down—his story of the war. (The account—highly recommended reading—he titled *Homage to Catalonia*.) In articles, he described a "reign of terror" under the communists. The pieces were turned down by *The New Statesman*, as was a book review of Franz Borkenau's *Spanish Cockpit*. The editors simply could not admit that their correspondents had been wrong. And they had been wrong. The POUM had nothing to do with Franco's forces, other than to fight them.

Victor Gollancz, who had published Orwell's *The Road to Wigan Pier* (with an advance of five hundred pounds, substantial for the time), rejected *Homage to Catalonia* out of hand. He turned it down in principle before a word had been written.

The point of all this is that Orwell, though a socialist, had committed the sin of belonging to the wrong faction. To the communists, this was unpardonable. Those who supported the communists justified the reign of terror. These apologists included W. H. Auden, whose poem *Spain* spoke of "necessary murder." Orwell could not tolerate the idea.

Death in battle was one thing, but cold-blooded murder, whether referred to as "liquidation of alien elements," was something else. He and Auden crossed swords, with the result that the poem was revised and eventually disowned.

Then, as now, it is not enough to urge reform (or even, for that matter, revolution) in, say, despotic Latin American countries. Nor will it do simply to fight for change. One must, above all else, be with the correct faction, the people with the most guns, which usually means the Soviet-supported group.

Why were the left-wing intellectuals so supportive of the communists and abusive of a fellow socialist like Orwell? They wanted to be on the winning side, as biographer Bernard Crick explains:

> Long before Orwell's difficulties in getting *Animal Farm* published in 1944, there were objective reasons to believe that many prominent Left-wing intellectuals were not as dedicated to truth and liberty as they were to the illusion of being close to the future levers of power if they kept the company of the Communists. Bertrand Russell accused them of worshipping the power as well as the sense of purpose in the Soviet Union. There is not the slightest ground for imputing persecution mania or paranoia to Orwell on this score. The socialist camp had gained as a recruit its most earnest and difficult free spirit.[6]

Though Orwell's before/after experience with communism is different than that of Fischer, Muggeridge, Koestler, and others, he definitely became a changed man after Spain. Thereafter, as he stated in *Why I Write*, he targeted every serious line he wrote against totalitarianism. The experiences in Catalonia, the jousts with the left-wing intelligentsia, and Orwell's dedication to the truth left a literary residue—*Animal Farm* and *1984*—which, thankfully, are still among the most-read novels of our time, even if they are banned or misinterpreted. As an example of the latter, to this day cover blurbs on *Animal Farm* state that the book is a "satire on dictatorship." Is it? Orwell described his own work as anti-Stalin, with no apologies. The British

Broadcasting Company in 1950 more accurately called it a satire on life in the Soviet Union. It bears repeating that fourteen publishers rejected this true work of genius. They could not bear the depiction of communist leaders as pigs.

Was Orwell one of those intellectuals—so numerous in Europe today—who say that the United States is as bad as the Soviet Union? (One notices with interest that they never reverse this statement.) Did he advocate unilateral nuclear disarmament? He cleared up his stance on these issues at a speech to a mostly communist audience at the Red Flag Fellowship in 1946.

> Orwell speculated about the possiblity of a world war between the USSR and the USA. The coming of an atom bomb might tempt either side into it. He argued clearly that it would be better to fight than go down; and that if there were such a war, he would choose to be on the side of America rather than Russia because, with all the faults of an uncontrolled capitalism, at least they had liberty. Where there was some liberty, it could be extended; but he took the view that the Soviet Union was so despotic that there was little hope of liberty even emerging there.[7]

The liberty Orwell cherished above all was liberty of thought. Writers who apologized for dictators he openly called bootlickers and whores. In 1948 he wrote to his publisher:

> I have just had Sartre's book on antisemitism, which you published, to review. I think Sartre is a bag of wind and I am going to give him a good boot.[8]

He saw the stakes clearly: the very existence of prose literature as such and, even, of those who wrote it—namely himself.

> But however it may be with the physical sciences, or with music, painting, and architecture, it is—as I have tried to show—certain that literature is doomed if liberty of thought perishes. Not only is it doomed in any country which retains a totalitarian structure; but any writer who adopts the totalitarian outlook, who finds excuses for persecution and the falsification of reality, thereby destroys himself as a writer.

There is no way out of this. No tirades against 'individualism' and 'the ivory tower', no pious platitudes to the effect that 'true individuality is only attained through identification with the community', can get over the fact that a bought mind is a spoiled mind. Unless spontaneity enters at some point or another, literary creation is impossible, and language itself becomes ossified. At some time in the future, if the human mind becomes something totally different from what it now is, we may learn to separate literary creation from intellectual honesty. At present we know only that the imagination, like certain wild animals, will not breed in captivity. Any writer or journalist who denies that fact—and nearly all the current praise of the Soviet Union contains or implies such a denial—is, in effect, demanding his own destruction.[9]

Orwell, like his friend Muggeridge, saw the death wish at work, implicit in the praise of totalitarian regimes. Though Muggeridge entertained few if any hopes of improvement in the situation, Orwell at least left valuable counsel. He recognized that no amount of logic or evidence from the most skilled debater can penetrate the dogmas of totalitarians. But that does not mean that one gives up. "There are certain people," Orwell told Stephen Spender, "like vegetarians and communists that one cannot answer. You just have to go on having your say regardless of them, and then the extraordinary thing is that they may start listening."[10]

CHAPTER 11, NOTES
1. Barbara Amiel, "Some Writers Are More Equal than Others," *Maclean's Magazine*, 18 May 1981, 52.
2. Bernard Crick, *George Orwell: A Life* (London: Secker and Warburg, 1980), 207.
3. Ibid., 3.
4. George Orwell, *Inside the Whale and Other Essays* (New York: Penguin Books, 1957), 153.
5. Crick, *George Orwell*, 219.
6. Ibid., 228.
7. Ibid., 341.
8. Ibid., 380.
9. Orwell, *Inside the Whale*, 174.
10. Crick, *George Orwell*, 404.

CHAPTER 12
PIERRE CHARETTE

P ierre Charette is not in the strictest sense a member of the generation that knew Joseph, even though Stalin died during his lifetime. Rather, he dealt with a Stalinist—Fidel Castro—and went not to the USSR but one of its colonies, which now very nearly may be called the Cuban Soviet Socialist Republic.

Canada has never broken diplomatic relations with Cuba, hence many Canadians visit the island. One, Pierre Charette, took a rather strange route. He also stayed a bit longer than the average tourist and did not spend all his time at the beach; hence, he merits special attention. But before delving into his extraordinary case, some background is necessary.

Quebec is a Canadian province. Its French-speaking inhabitants are not Frenchmen, they are Quebecois— French-speaking North Americans. The long history of these people is widely ignored, but not nearly so much as the recent past, in spite of important developments.

Possessing a different language and culture from the rest of North America has led a great number of Quebecois in the direction of political independence. When Charles de Gaulle shouted *Vive le Québec libre!* on a trip to the province, he did not create the desire for independence, he merely played to it. The *Parti Québécois*, elected in 1976, held and lost a referendum on sovereignty-association, a position once compared by former Prime Minister Pierre Trudeau to an adolescent who wanted to live on his own, but insisted at the same time that his parents foot the bills. In any case, the *Parti Québécois* saw no reason why a confederation put together by wigged men with quills cannot be peacefully dissolved by modern men in suits writing with ballpoints. But they practice diplomacy.

Other groups have taken a different approach. They not only want a total break from Canada but from Western Democracy as well. Pierre Charette, born in 1943, belonged to one of these.

A former disc jockey on Radio Canada, Charette was a *felquiste*, a member of *Le Front de Libération du Québec* (FLQ), a group similar to the American Weather Underground and Black Panthers, with whom they cooperated. René Lévesque, premier of Quebec, once described FLQ philosophy as "kindergarten Marxism." They rode the wave of student protest in the sixties, affirming the entire Marxist creed, including the belief that North American consumer capitalism was moribund and oppressive and that the future belonged to socialism. To *Québec libre!* they would add, *Québec socialiste!* But they did more than protest. For them the spirit, at least, of the biblical text applied—faith without works is dead.

The FLQ publicized manifestos and blew up buildings. In what became known as the October Crisis of 1970, they kidnapped British trade commissioner James Cross and Quebec labor minister Pierre Laporte, murdering the latter. Pierre Trudeau, a man of socialist inclinations who often praised Mao Tse-tung, imposed martial law.

Charette, pursued by the police for his suspected involvement in three bombings, fled to New York and into hiding with the Black Panthers. On 5 March 1969, he and companion Alain Allard hijacked an Eastern Airlines jet en route to Miami, directing the craft to Havana.

Charette described the following ten years in the book *Mes Dix Années D'exil à Cuba* ("My Ten Years of Exile in Cuba"), unfortunately unavailable in English. His sojourn is particularly valuable because those disillusioned by Cuban realities are less numerous than the earlier Russophiles. Charette can thus be compared with an earlier generation.

One would assume that someone from the front lines such as Charette, who had actually begun the demolition of capitalism with real dynamite, would be hailed as hero and role model in Cuba, or at least be made to feel at home. But things did not turn out that way. In the early going, Charette and Allard were held practically under house arrest in a hotel, to the point where they were forced not only to write a desperate appeal to Fidel Castro but to begin a hunger strike just to get attention. When they asked what would be done with them, they were informed they had the right to ask questions, but their hosts had the right not to answer.

> It is necessary to say that, arriving in that paradise of dogma, intransigence, and forced labor that a socialist country like Cuba was at that time, and still remains, young idealist that I was, I received a rather violent shock. All my dreams of social liberation and individual emancipation crumbled in a matter of months.[1]

How could someone at the beginning of his revolutionary career change so (pardon the expression) radically? Apparently the Cuba that protesters raved about, where Susan Sontag affirmed in 1968 that people refused to sleep in order to work around the clock for the revolution,[2] was nowhere to be found. The kingdom of happy, willing workers, the abolition of unemployment, abundance for everyone, complete freedom—in short, every good thing—that others had discovered existed only, Charette discovered, in their illusions. For the elite and the admirers, Cuba was a legend in its own mind, a shadow of its future self.

Charette and Allard realized that they would be used as political pawns, but they had few alternatives. They would have to play the game. The logic of planning soon became evident.

Language training came first. Charette acquired complete fluency and used his new abilities to read such works as Colombian Gabriel Garcia Márquez's *A Hundred Years of Solitude*. But actual solitude eluded him. Apparently at the time, foreigners in Cuba, whatever their degree of orthodoxy, were subjected to classes of communist catechism involving daily discussions of Marx, Lenin and Stalin. The dialogue did not include disagreements with these venerable gentlemen. For these special classes, Charette did not even have to ask. In a socialist country, as everyone knows, education is not only free but compulsory.

Certain Cubans, he found, were still ardent True Believers in the New Faith. Charette describes Roberto, an old-style communist doctor who maintained a vision of a sparkling, classless future where the state would indeed fade away. It may be an example of Blake's Fearful Symmetry that the man was also physically blind. Had he been able to see the evidence, he may have taken the route of other Cubans.

Wilfredo, the group leader, appeared to be the absolute master of the Sacred Texts, able to quote chapter and verse with ease. How much stock he actually put in them became apparent when he obtained permission to visit his Russian fiancée in Mexico for fifteen days. He never returned. Charette, perhaps taking note of this, determined to one day get out. But with security personnel on every hand, this would be no easy task.

For one thing, the Cuban authorities stuck Charette along with other foreigners on a nearby island. Charette later described this group—idealistic Swedes, Black Panthers, disgruntled businessmen, Italian communists, a tuba-playing American—as a veritable insane asylum. Why the isolation? Charette charges the Castro regime with xenophobia, quarantining its inmates from contamination by foreigners. A kind of apartheid system is thus enforced. Cuban officials subtly expressed doubts about Charette's morality, though in his view they had no right to judge, especially since some of the racy cabaret acts deemed immoral under Batista received full party support once nationalized.

The incarceration on the island effectively paralyzed the young radical. But a salvation of sorts appeared. In socialist countries, whoever does not work does not eat. Come what may, full employment prevails. *Granma* is *the* journal of Cuba, a Caribbean *Pravda* no more lively than the Russian version. Charette was assigned to the publication as a translator.

In pre-Cuba days, Charette had scoffed at *Reader's Digest* when it attacked socialist countries and their alleged brainwashing practices. Pure establishment propaganda, he thought. But he quickly discovered that the rule at *Granma* was to blindly defend the revolution, whatever the facts.[3] If *Máximo Líder* Fidel decreed that two plus two equals five, it would have to run that way.

> At *Granma* I vegetated; an ectoplasm, a zombie! Little by little, that's what I was becoming on an intellectual level. By daily translating the same insipidities, by rereading the same cliches and by continuously trotting out the same irrelevancies, I had acquired a perfectly mechanical style which perfectly filled the demands of a cheap propaganda organ. . . . *Granma* is an empty journal, and I wore myself out translating the empty articles of empty journalists.[4]

Such was the torpor at *Granma* that when Charette's health failed and he had to enter the hospital, he considered it a day of rejoicing.

While Charette's experiences did not lead him to turn to any traditional religious faith, he saw the prevailing Cuban theology all too clearly.

> Men pass away; the Party is immortal. The Party is God the Father, the Supreme Being. Castro? He is Robespierre all over again. One could just as well have been in the France of 1789.[5]

He noticed too that organizations such as the CTC (*Central de Trabajadores de Cuba*) and the CDR (*Comité por la*

Defensa de la Revolución) engaged primarily in surveillance and denunciation, a kind of permanent, institutionalized McCarthyism. Or, if you will, an Inquisition.

> Their official role: to mobilise, mobilise. . . . The real function? Maintain surveillance and denounce. The citizens are thus controlled twenty-four hours a day by these two organizations, the CTC and the CDR.[6]

And those who commit one of the multitudinous crimes against the state? Charette's descriptions of Cuban prisons contrast sharply with those of the veterans of guided tours of special show facilities.

> In [Canada] prison strips a person of his liberty—to be sure, a terrible punishment. But prison in Cuba is synonymous with the total annihilation of the individual.[7]

Geo, a Salvadoran comrade, stumbled inadvertently on a concentration camp setup that reminded him of similar arrangements under the Nazis: barbed wire, shaved heads, guard dogs, heavily armed soldiers holding vigil from towers. The discovery did not astound Charette.

> Poor Geo! He did not yet understand that the whole island was nothing more than an immense concentration camp, where the prisons served as dungeons for those with the hardest heads.[8]

Neither could Cuba's preponderant military might be hidden. Charette describes Cuba as "completely militarized." This posed dilemmas for the country's youth.

> Certain adolescents viewed their approaching military service with a spirit of outrage, since it would deprive them of the morsel of liberty they had and transform them into robots in a system that had designated their place since birth. But, of course, the sons of the government officials managed to escape it. Their country was at war: it would always be at war. All through their childhood they had been drenched in militarism and war psychosis. What happens today will remain true for future generations who will play war games with their toy revolvers, machine guns, arrows and swords.[9]

The human spirit is such that, even under difficult conditions, normal relations and friendships can be possible. For Charette, Cuba was not entirely a vale of tears, although his positive experiences came in spite of the Castro regime. He expressed thankfulness that at least the party had not been able to nationalize and ration the sun. The descriptions of his friends Fidelito and Dinorah are poignant. They resemble, after a fashion, the prison relationships described by Solzhenitsyn. Doubtless, they helped him maintain a handhold on sanity.

But with or without genuine friends, Charette longed to get out. His illusions had long since died. The game had gone into overtime. He resigned from *Granma* and announced his intention to return to Canada.

The true test of a totalitarian regime, however, is not how easy it is to get in but how easily one gets out. It took nearly two years. They brought various pressures on him to stay. That they let him out at all represents a minor miracle. With what sort of political beliefs did he leave?

> After ten years, I openly support the freedom of our democracy against the oppression of the Cuban *granias*—that is, gulags.[10]

Returning home, Charette confessed a certain pride in being Canadian and an admiration for his country's diplomats. (Though he still seeks independence for Québec, he would favor the Canadian governmental model.) But there was the sticky matter of those bombings and the hijacked plane. Many times, Charette would have gladly exchanged his 3,545 days in Cuba for a stint in any of the Quebec jails—some of the worst in Canada but hotels by Cuban standards. He got his wish. The following words were written in Bordeaux prison, 21 May 1979:

> Physically aged, I was nonetheless conscious of reawakening to life, despite the uncertainties of my future. I'm firmly convinced that I can never again repeat the same errors, for

which I paid in suffering and humiliation. . . . I returned culturally and politically enriched among my people, who have also matured. Filled with a new energy, I felt the obligation to pursue my struggle for the true liberty.[11]

May God grant that he finds it, in every sense. At least he knows where not to look.

CHAPTER 12, NOTES
1. Pierre Charette, *Mes Dix Années D'exil à Cuba* (Montreal: Editions Stanké, 1979), 10. Translation by Marie-Jeanne Dupuis.
2. Paul Hollander, *Political Pilgrims* (New York: Oxford University Press, 1981), 245.
3. In his comments on *Reader's Digest*, Charette has gained recent support. Susan Sontag claimed in 1981 that one could learn more about the true nature of communism from *Reader's Digest* than *The Nation*, a standard of the American left.
4. Charette, *Mes Dix Années*, 143, 144.
5. Ibid., 150.
6. Ibid., 116.
7. Ibid., 153.
8. Ibid., 155.
9. Ibid., 87-88.
10. Ibid., 12.
11. Ibid., 249.

CHAPTER 13
HONORABLE MENTION

In the thirties, the Future was socialist stock; the Bolsheviks were selling shares. One of the most willing buyers was Louis Fischer, an American journalist born of Russian parents.

An admirer of Peter Kroptkin, a nobleman turned anarchist, Fischer could not understand why anyone would deride the efforts of a great nation to pull itself out of its ugly past. It seemed to him that for the first time, a government sought to fulfill the dreams of all the reformers down through the ages. He held no doubts about Soviet sincerity and in his journalistic role became one of the regime's most shameless propagandists.

One of the original contributors to *The God That Failed*, Fischer eventually became disgusted with Stalin, whom he called the Supreme Slave Master. Around the time of the Ukraine famine, Fischer realized that he was glorifying factories, dams, and other symbols of Progress, and forgetting human beings. The Nazi-Soviet pact proved more than his political faith could handle, and he apostatized.

Thereafter, Fischer derived his wisdom from Gandhi, whose biography he wrote. (The book was used in making the award-winning film *Ghandi*. Fischer's *Life of Lenin* won a

National Book Award in 1964.) In later years, Fischer compared the Soviet Union to a gigantic company town from which there was no escape. The great Soviet promise of the future, in his view, amounted to little more than a large chunk of humanity adapting the language of the Sunday afternoon soapbox orator. Fischer held that the difficulties of a free society could be overcome, but left this haunting question—what can Soviet citizens do about Stalinism? To date the answer appears to be, nothing.

Freda Utley, raised in the best British tradition, is certainly worthy of inclusion in the ranks of dissenters. An intellectual and writer of note, she authored *Japan's Feet Of Clay* and *Last Chance In China,* among other books. She became a communist in the belief that the writings of Marx and Lenin, like those of Shelley, Swinburne, and even Pericles, led to the emancipation of mankind. Later, like Koestler, she realized that communism provided a substitute for religion. With Arcadi, her Russian husband, she went to the Soviet Union to throw in her lot with the people. The account of her gradual awakening to the truth, her disillusionment and complete change of heart is found in her book *Lost Illusion,* a detailed, powerful work. Her husband likewise realized that Stalinism was a brutal hoax. In 1936 the secret police arrested him. Freda Utley never saw him again. As Koestler described, she carried his shroud as her banner for the rest of her life.

The following year, the show trials and purges in the Soviet Union were in full swing. Back in England, Orwell was being called a liar and a fascist. Malcolm Muggeridge was still reeling in his soul from his Moscow experiences. In fact, he thought he might have left his soul there. What had happened to the land of Tolstoy, Turgenev, Chekhov, Gogol, and so many others? Along with the most basic human rights, had the dictatorship of the proletariat abolished their kind as well? Certainly the Stalinist regime had not, indeed could not, produce anything that would pass for art. On 17

July 1937 Muggeridge wrote an article in *Time and Tide* called "Men and Books." It contained these words:

> Perhaps a new literature will come to pass in Russia, as one did in the darkest days of Tsarist repression. If so, it will be a literature of revolt and so anathema to the Soviet Establishment. Perhaps it is being furtively scribbled even now in concentration camps and other dark corners. . . . Not even Dialectical Materialism, not even that, can put out the light of genius.[1]

As it turned out, this article was prophetically true on several counts: dialectical materialism, thankfully, has not been able to extinguish genius (or Christianity); a new literature was, even then, being furtively scribbled in concentration camps; and lastly, this literature was anathema to the Soviet establishment.

The Soviet bosses erred terribly when they jailed a young army officer named Aleksandr Solzhenitsyn for making unflattering remarks about Stalin in a letter. *The Gulag Archipelago, One Day in the Life of Ivan Denisovich*, and the rest of the literary yield of his imprisonment turned a whole generation of French intellectuals away from socialism.

Bernard-Henri Lévy, who participated in the Paris student riots of 1968, said that he had learned more from Solzhenitsyn than from many "totalitarian" languages. This is probably a reference to what Arthur Koestler dubbed "Dzhugashvilese," a dialect that currently exists in many tongues, a kind of para-Marxist Esperanto used by Western apologists and Eastern bloc pitchmen.

"Socialism with a human face" was the latest creation of the totalitarian dialect, though then, as now, it was nowhere in evidence. Lévy accordingly titled his book *Barbarism with a Human Face*. In it he attacked what he called the lies of "red fascism," proclaiming Marxist regimes the most repressive of all. The gulag system of prison camps, far from being an accident, were in his view integral to the system.

Lévy and colleagues like André Glucksmann say in often rather dense and academic prose the obvious: Marxism is bad. Apply it in any country you want and the result will be gulag in the end. Collectivism, a classless society, socialism—all are impossible without terror. There are surely many other reasons for their change of heart, but Solzhenitsyn is foremost among them. And like Solzhenitsyn, Lévy and Glucksmann are scorned by Western liberals, if they are known at all. Illusions die hard.

Still others had to learn by direct experience. Eldridge Cleaver, for instance, sojourned in various Third World Marxist states, including Cuba. Once a socialist fundamentalist, he now completely repudiates the left. But his story is well known.

There are others, such as Djilas or the Russian Victor Kravchenko (author of *I Choose Freedom*) from the government ranks. Carlos Franqui and Huber Matos were former colleagues of Fidel Castro. A whole string of socialist diplomats have recently defected, including two of Nicaragua's ambassadors to the United States.

All these people, and others like them, have their own story to tell. The evidence is there. All one has to do is search it out. But the desire to do that has been little in evidence.

In the case of ideological refugees from places such as, say, Chile or Argentina, the victims are readily accorded celebrity status and encouraged to "speak out" against the military junta. Jacobo Timmerman is an example of such a person. But "speaking out" against communist regimes very nearly disqualifies one from a hearing. It is labeled "stridency" or "bitterness," evidence that the experiences—of Solzhenitsyn for instance—have made him an "extremist" or "unbalanced."

Much credit is due for those intellectuals who remained steady and clearheaded vis-à-vis totalitarianism through the bulk of this insane century. Bertrand Russell is one of these, even if one does not care for the majority of his views. French philosopher Raymond Aron is another. His case is remarkable because of the strong popularity of the left, headed by Sartre, in France. The religious community was not all composed of Hewlett Johnsons. Reinhold Niebuhr and Dietrich Bonhoeffer, for example, took a strong stand against the new tyrannies.

The tragedy, though, is that totalitarian spokesmen have had better, as it were, amplification systems than the above witnesses. They have never hesitated to state their case, with the volume turned on full. One can hear them still.

CHAPTER 13, NOTES
1. Ian Hunter, *Malcolm Muggeridge: A Life* (Nashville: Nelson, 1980), 90.

PART

2

THE GENERATION
THAT KNEW NOT JOSEF

*Rien de plus dangereux, qu'une idée générale dans des cerveaux étroits et vides
(There is nothing more dangerous than a general idea in empty, narrow minds).*
                                                            Hippolyte Taine

*What the recent Polish events illustrate is a truth that we should have understood
a very long time ago: that communism is fascism.*   Susan Sontag

SECTION 1
DUPLICATION

FIRST CHURCH OF CHRIST SOCIALIST

The churches feel bound to proclaim a better world, thereby promoting their own extinction.   Malcolm Muggeridge

Though Stalin is dead, his system lives on in every Marxist dictatorship. In every place where this kind of regime exists, the results have been the same: poverty, death, hunger, a new and terrible feudalism, and refugees who flee on foot, hide in the wheel wells of airplanes, float to freedom on inner tubes, or, in the case of one German family, fly to safety in a makeshift hot-air balloon.

We have seen nearly seventy years of the new theocratic rule in countries from Russia to Cuba to Kampuchea. It has involved famines, persecutions, the loss of the most basic human rights, invasions, the removal of native people from their homes, threats, purges, and executions numbering well into the millions. Historically, these crimes and losses have been irreversible. No Marxist theocracy has ever evolved into a more liberal regime or been overthrown.

In view of all this and more, it takes a special kind of person to duplicate the earlier record of servile apology toward Marxist dictatorships, coupled with an antagonism toward the West. Considering the record, one would think that some sort of objectivity bypass surgery would be necessary for this activity. Sadly, this is not the case. In, of all

places, the Christian church—even its evangelical sectors—
people may be found who are very much up to the task.

This group is wonderfully like their spiritual patriarchs
Hewlett Johnson and Anna Louise Strong. Though they
think of themselves as radical and the purveyors of something new, they are quite rigidly traditional, following in the
footsteps of their spiritual and political forebearers. This du-
plication of the earlier record happens everywhere two or
three gather together to apologize for totalitarianism.

One of the few areas where the two groups differ is that
Strong and her flock went and lived in the actual countries
they thought so superior to their own. In contrast, the
socialist evangelicals' line is, "Yes, they have a just society,
but I don't want to live there." Except for the occasional in-
dulgence in a bit of political tourism—traveling to some
Marxist country at the behest of the government and there
denouncing their own country—they have pretty much remained in the United States, marketing their ideology like
regular capitalist publishers. Like William F. Buckley's *National Review*, they even appeal for donations. Public relations firms have written some of their appeal letters. *Dear
friend, are you content to sit still while the generals plot and the
people go hungry? If not then you should subscribe to . . .* that
sort of thing. Jim Wallis, editor of *Sojourners* magazine and a
leader of the radical Christian movement, has even mar-
keted his autobiography *Revive Us Again: A Sojourner's
Story*, very much in the style of similar volumes about con-
verted film stars or athletes. In addition, the magazine once
offered Richard Barnet's *Global Reach* as a bonus incentive to
subscribers.

Another difference is that, in the thirties, the West did
seem moribund and the socialist regimes indeed appeared to
be the wave of the future. They were new at the time, hence
Strong, John Reed, and others had some legitimate excuses,
at least at the very beginning. Now the failure of socialism is
manifest everywhere it has been tried. As Koestler said, it is
all as if none of this happened, such are the repetition of the

earlier errors. This time, the writer of *Darkness at Noon* said, there can be no pardon.

Opening up a bit, one might say generally that the religious left, including the radical revivalists, liberal Protestants, the World Council of Churches, the Catholic activists, and groups within the Anabaptist churches are doing a good job of duplicating the earlier record. It is a weakness to which, for some reason, the religious mind is prone. This study will focus primarily on the leftist evangelicals.

It will be surely objected that terms such as "evangelical left," "radical Christian," "religious left," or "socialists" constitute a demeaning labeling of others. Is this a legitimate complaint? I don't think so.

People on the left like to say that they reject labels. What this means is that they reject labels for themselves while freely tagging others "reactionaries" or "right wing," even if their political tenets are those of the Western, democratic mainstream. Even "capitalist" and "conservative" are used as pejorative labels. No apology is necessary for referring to people whose agenda mirrors—or even exceeds—the partisan left as either "socialist" or the "religious left" or what they say they are—radical Christians.

One should say at the outset that to point out that Jesus, during his stay on earth, refused to ally himself to radical causes like Jewish nationalism and the overthrow of the Romans, that he spoke often of the delusions and sorrows of this world, and that he resolutely proclaimed his Kingdom "not of this world" does little good today. To believe this is to stand accused of peddling religious opium.

In the *Screwtape Letters*, C. S. Lewis portrays the diabolical strategy as changing the various versions of Jesus every few decades. About ten years ago the Revolutionary Christ was in vogue, sort of a Jesus as a first-century, Marxist-dialoguing, Jesuit, liberation theologian, complete with parachute, grenades, and loaded AK-47. Currently nothing, it appears, can keep Jesus from being enlisted as the Democratic Socialist candidate for the 25th Congressional district, running on a social justice ticket, concerned about militarism (Western) and North-South dialogue. Why, if Jesus was not actually a paid-up member of Greenpeace and a regular shouter at antinuke rallies, it is only because neither nuclear power nor that organization existed at the time; otherwise, he surely would have been a card-carrying member. Had Nestle sold infant formula in Nazareth, he surely would have led the boycott of that company. While an earlier group made a god out of socialism, the new version proclaims God to be a socialist.

Of course, it is never stated quite this way. Ron Sider, another radical Christian leader, speaks constantly of "biblical norms" for social justice. Asked if these norms are the same for conservative Republicans as they are for liberal Democrats, Sider replies, "The Bible does not have an economic blueprint for the modern economy or a political platform for the next presidential candidate." But in the next breath, he declares that, "God wills structural mechanisms which tend to reduce the extremes of wealth and poverty."[1]

The whole bent of Sider, and soi-disant radical publications such as *Sojourners* and the *Other Side*, is that capitalism, particularly as it exists in the United States, is an insidious evil, an "oppressive system." One can only conclude that these "structural mechanisms" are based on the socialist model. The conclusion is warranted since the religious left makes a point of defending Third World Marxist regimes and attacking the United States and Western Europe.

This was not always so. The *Other Side*, before 1970, was called *Freedom Now*. The writing of Joseph Bayly and the late Francis Schaeffer appeared regularly in its pages. But not now. Today, one is more likely to find a vitriolic denunciation of the Wycliffe Bible Translators as a CIA front, or the Salvation Army dismissed as hopelessly allied to the status quo because business leaders sit on its board.

Instead of following the biblical injunction for just

weights and a just balance, the socialist evangelicals have two moral measuring systems: a lenient one for socialists and a strict one for everybody else, particularly the United States.[2] Respected theologian Clark Pinnock, once a *Sojourners* contributing editor, has severed association with the publication for precisely these reasons, particularly anti-Americanism. His articles, such as "Marxism, The Opium of the People"[3] never found favor there anyway, for obvious reasons.

Although Third World Marxist dictatorships—not the USSR—are the religious left's Buffalo Bill (their idol or role model), there is at least one example of a theologian who sees merit in, yes, Joseph Stalin.

José Míguez Bonino, from Argentina, is the author of *Christians and Marxists: The Mutual Challenge to Revolution.* He begins his chapter "Communist Heros" by equating Christian spirituality with Marxist militancy. Stalin is his first hero. Reading the biography of Stalin, he says, made a "deep impression" on him. He briefly acknowledges Stalin's faults in terms that border on euphemism: callousness, hatred, cynicism; then adds:

> He will grasp for power (and use it) unashamedly. He will destroy, bend, overpower. He can be ruthless and cold. But one feels always in the presence of a man who, in his innermost being, has given himself to a cause, which is not always very clear and well defined (and therefore quite frequently turned into his own whim), but which masters his whole life. There is no frivolity, no equivocation, no possible relativising of this commitment. What ever else he may be, he is—subjectively—a 'militant.'[4]

Remember that Bonino has previously legitimized this militant concept as approximating Christian spirituality. He carries on:

> I have chosen a rather perverse example, because it seems to me to indicate that communism, even at its worst, displays a depth which we cannot ignore. There is a seriousness which reminds us of the Puritan concentration on 'the one thing that matters', the exclusion of all that is superfluous or

> distracting in terms of the one purpose and goal. There is a
> total subordination of subjectivity and subjective feeling:
> Love, family, artistic or emotional satisfaction, even one's
> own life and security—everything is 'counted as loss' for the
> sake of the cause. Sometimes we shudder at the ruthlessness
> of this total concentration.[5]

If Bonino and his fellow liberation theologians cannot
ignore Stalin's "depth" and "shudder at the ruthlessness of
this total concentration," so, doubtless, did untold
thousands in the gulag.

To show the seriousness of this, imagine for a moment
someone like Bonino, a Christian living comfortably in the
West, writing something in this vein: "May I comment on
the deep impression Hitler made upon me. Hitler can be
ruthless and cold. But one feels always in the presence of a
man who, in his innermost being, has given himself to a
cause. He was cynical, yes, but he shows a depth we cannot
ignore."

Rev. Hewlett Johnson in his day credited Hitler for understanding that Judaism and Christianity find their fulfillment in socialism and communism. But he reserved his admiration for Stalin, based on his greater militancy. Like
Bonino, he decided to go with a winner.

Examples of the same abound in the religious left.
Daniel Berrigan, another contributing editor to *Sojourners*,
found the face of Ho Chi Minh reminiscent of Jesus Christ.
With the Sandinista junta, currently the most popular
theocracy, the hagiography is laid on in thick gobs. In the
minds of their foreign admirers, if they are not quite the
representatives of Jesus Christ himself, well, they are the
closest thing possible. "Sandinism" has replaced
"Dzugashvilese" as a dialect.

To many people, Christian and otherwise, this sort of
thing is worthy of ridicule. Orwell turned his powers of in-
vective on it. Malcolm Muggeridge has laughed at it for
years. The *Wittenburg Door* parodied radical Christians in a
spoof called "Sobouring." Why bother, then, with some-

thing so palpably ludicrous? There are a number of reasons why the religious left deserves study.

As mentioned earlier in the chapter on Muggeridge, the church associates wisdom with solemnity. Increasingly, the evangelical community takes the *Sojourners* mentality seriously, to the point that it is widely thought that the majority of professors of social ethics in seminaries adhere to a leftist line. One reason for the popularity of radical Christianity among academics and students is that journals like *Sojourners* imply that to be on the left is to be intelligent and to be otherwise is reactionary and unintelligent. Malcolm Muggeridge once wrote that for the most part, the reverse was true.[6]

Evangelicals, after decades of hibernation, have had their political consciousness raised and there is a battle going on for loyalties. They now realize that, as Orwell said, there is no such thing as, "staying out of politics." But, at present, to be politically aware or socially active is automatically assumed to mean an inclination to the left. Evangelicals are great faddists, and this is one more fad, as other signs show.

His, the magazine of Inter-Varsity Christian Fellowship, devoted eight pages, a full 25 percent of a thirty-two page issue (January 1984) to what amounted to a free political advertisement for the Nicaraguan government. Junta members, including Daniel Ortega (appropriately shown in military uniform), were given carte blanche to express their views with only the mildest criticism of their policies allowed. In addition, *His* advertised a Nicaraguan information packet, decidedly slanted in the direction of the junta. *His* had never done anything remotely approaching this before, as several readers were quick to point out in subsequent issues.

The religious left, specifically *Sojourners*, regularly thunders against mainstream Americans as being greedy, materialistic, racist, idolatrous supporters of an oppressive status quo. Yet at the same time, they have somehow escaped the scrutiny they so readily apply, in the name of Jesus

Christ, to everyone else. Evangelical leaders for their part have been quite generous with them, to the point that *Sojourners* promotional literature includes blurbs like "tough investigative journalism" from people such as Carl Henry and Kenneth Kantzer.

Following the "Sobouring" satire in the *Wittenburg Door*, the *Door* editors received a lengthy epistle from *Sojourners* brass who, to put it mildly, were not amused. They apparently thought that televised faith healers were fair game for satire, but not them. While other *Door* bull's-eyes such as Hal Lindsey have shown the ability to laugh at themselves, not so *Sojourners*. Whoever tackles them can expect to earn their unalloyed wrath, which might be the best indicator of how on target one has been. Should they label the critic "right wing" or "far right," chances are he has hit home. The point of all this is that the religious left knows how to dish out, but not how to take.

In the case of *Sojourners*, the publication is the house journal of their semimonastic urban ministry. At one time their masthead flaunted the fact that they held all things in common, while being allowed fifteen dollars a month spending money. Joseph Bayly smuggled a reference to such evangelical neomonasticism into his novel *Winterflight*. There is something very South African about a tiny, aloof community radically separated from the everyday life of the mainstream, launching jeremiads against the populace; along, of course, with appeals to buy their books, donate money, and subscribe to their magazine.

In a controlled society, immunity from criticism is possible, but not in a free one. While there have been a number of books analyzing the neoconservative movement—with question-begging titles like *Greed Is Not Enough*—and many works attacking what has become known as the "religious right," critical studies of the religious left have been rare. The Christian socialists have become something of a sacred cow. I agree with Mike Yaconelli who wrote that the radical Christian movement is "far from infallible" and "subject to criticism like everybody else."[7] It is time to provide what has been neglected in the past. It is an act of affirmative action.

CHAPTER 14, NOTES
1. "An Interview with Ron Sider," *The Wittenburg Door,* November 1979, 12.
2. Lloyd Billingsley, "First Church of Christ Socialist," *National Review,* 28 October 1983, 1339.
3. Clark Pinnock, "Marxism, the Opium of the People," *Christianity Today,* 7 August 1981, 51. *See also* "A Political Pilgrimage," *Eternity,* October 1984, 26-29.
4. José Míguez Bonino, *Christians and Marxists* (London: Hodder and Stoughton, 1976), 134.
5. Ibid.
6. Malcolm Muggeridge, *Like It Was: The Diaries of Malcolm Muggeridge* (New York: Morrow, 1982), 386.
7. Mike Yaconelli, "The Back Door," *The Wittenburg Door,* November 1979, 32.

CHAPTER 15
THE ALIBI ARMORY

THE USSR

The religious left, particularly *Sojourners* and the *Other Side*, do not break into rhapsodies over Soviet economics as Anna Louise Strong did when she spoke of a five-year plan "bursting forth from the loins of a hundred and sixty million people." They do not maintain, as she did, that in the USSR the jails were so humane that criminals actually applied for admittance and had to be pleaded with to leave when their term had expired. Neither can they match Rev. Hewlett Johnson's great one-liners about the humble man Stalin bringing in the kingdom of Christ, and his Soviet regime being the "salvation of the world." Neither have any of them, to my knowledge, renounced their citizenship, forsaken the idolatrous, materialistic United States, and gone to become part of the Great Social Experiment. There may well be some, though.

The religious left sometimes acknowledges that the USSR is repressive, its economy a failure, and its allure in the rest of the world largely diminished. But whatever the difficulties, much of it is largely the fault of the United States and the West. Radical Christians, like their ideological ancestors, continue to apologize for the Soviet Union.

"Conflict between the U.S. and the Soviet Union," writes Danny Collum, "has never been inevitable."[1] Collum makes no comment about Lenin's view that antagonism between the good, revolutionary countries (USSR) and the bad, capitalistic, bourgeois countries (USA) was just that— inevitable until the good guys won. Didn't some people, in the theocratic view, have to be "eliminated as a class"? Since no attempt is made to deal with these precepts which are, after all, the very foundation of Soviet expansionism, we are left wondering if Collum considers the current Soviet bosses cool pragmatists who don't believe that stuff anymore. "At each step in the Cold War," he says, having stated earlier that the cold war was essentially the fault of the West, "the U.S. was presented with a choice between very different but equally plausible interpretations of Soviet intentions . . . at every turn U.S. policy-makers have chosen to assume the very worst about the Soviet Counterparts."

And why not? After internal repression and even genocide, forced labor, persecution of minorities and religious believers, tossing of dissidents into insane asylums, an alliance with Nazi Germany, the annexation of the Baltic states, the direct control of Eastern Europe, direct threats ("We will bury you!" Remember?), and much more, what was a policymaker to think? That he was dealing with an amiable parliamentary democracy?

These things, Collum continues, were not the actual reasons for U.S. concern. No, "what really provoked fear and military response was the revolution's expropriation of property and redistribution of wealth." Even though expropriation of property and redistribution of wealth are impossible without terror (and, incidentally, are also the policy of burglars), Collum evidently approves, because instead of discussing the morality of these measures he continues with a litany of American sins. It is a given with radical Christians that one never criticizes socialism in principle.

On the subject of the Soviet invasion of Afghanistan, the same writer says, "The Soviet invasion of Afghanistan is

an international crime" (the reader, used to the usual
Sojourner's line, begins to wonder if there is something wrong
here—but he is not disappointed for long) "whose only equal
may be the slaughter the United States is funding in Central
America."[2] There you have it, just weights and a just balance.

Here is Jim Wallis's RIP on Leonid Brezhnev in the December 1982 *Sojourners*: "If we could not call Brezhnev a
peacemaker, we could at least recognize him as a moderate
man, a man open to reason."[3] Did Brezhnev deploy SS-20s?
Invade Afghanistan? Repress Sakharov and other dissidents?
No matter, he was someone who "genuinely desired peace."
The latter statement is nearly identical to Rev. Johnson's
pronouncements on Stalin. He would be proud of his disciple.

Anyone whose relatives were murdered in the downing
of Korean Airlines flight 007 (269 killed) in August 1983
will doubtless be relieved to know that *Sojourners* considers
this to be a "tragic blunder" followed by a "callous cover-up."[4] "But Soviet leaders," the piece carries on, "were
genuinely and understandably bewildered by the unusually
vicious and frenzied name-calling that came from the United
States in the wake of the tragedy." Notice the term "tragedy"
which disinfects the deed of moral implications. The Soviet
action was a "blunder," a tactical term; the resulting name-calling by the West was "vicious," a value-loaded word. Now
why would anyone whose relatives had been needlessly murdered want to do something as wicked as call the murderers
names?

Observe, too, how the Soviet leaders were "understandably bewildered." There is a certain accuracy to this.
The lives of mere innocent human beings have never caused
the dictatorship of the proletariat to get all worked up. Why
should it do so to anyone else? What was all the fuss about?
Why, they were just bewildered.

(By the way, the worst name-calling came not from the
United States but from France where headlines appeared

containing descriptions like *Camarade Folamour* ["Comrade Strangelove"] for the Soviet leader who ordered the plane to be shot down.)

But the rule for radical Christians is: any criticism of the Soviet Union must be immediately followed by a similar or more severe criticism of the United States. The socialist system itself is off limits.

Jim Wallis also overflowed with compassion for the victims of the "tragedy." He identifies the root causes of the 269 deaths:

> However, we must all be extremely careful lest we become so self-righteous in our own indignation and anger over this incident that we become guilty of hypocrisy. The root causes of these tragic deaths are to be found in the pervasive climate of fear, distrust, and hostility that has been allowed to develop among many nations. But in particular, the poisoned relations between ourselves and the Soviet Union have created a virtual war mentality. The passengers aboard flight 007 were clearly victims of that mentality. The Soviet Union is responsible for the murders of these people, but we must also share the guilt. On such a dark day, none of us is innocent."[5]

On a matter of such gravity, any writer should speak for himself. If Wallis feels guilty for an act perpetrated by the Soviet government, that is his problem. I do not feel any such guilt; I feel outrage. To tell the relatives of these murdered people—many of them were children—that "we must also share the guilt," can hardly be construed as a message of comfort. If this were not enough, Wallis charges others with being "ideologues."

Regarding the persecution of religious believers in the Soviet Union, two American church leaders recently assailed Russian Christians who unfurled banners reading, "This is a persecuted Church," during a worship service in Moscow.[6] Instead of taking up the issue of human rights with their hosts, the visitors were "offended" by the protest and accused the demonstrators of "trying to grab media attention." One member of the visiting group said that if the protesters wanted to discuss human rights, they should have arranged a meeting with the U.S. delegation. The remarks astonished members of the diplomatic community who are well aware of the restrictions on religion imposed by the Soviet state, which has recently stiffened penalties for citizens who try to contact foreigners. Dr. Bruce Rigdon, who heads the National Council of Churches committee on relations with Soviet churches, commented that "this also happens in the United States." Rev. John Lindner held up a photograph of a Soviet church under construction. He "had heard of a couple of instances of new churches being built." We are not told if he had seen them.

Thus, with the USSR, the religious left will allow a certain amount of criticism, usually followed by an assertion that the United States is just as bad. (As mentioned earlier, one notices that the order is never reversed.) The criticism never questions the legitimacy of socialism and is kept within the same limits—"blunders," "mistakes," and so on—as Soviet publications themselves. It is all very Johnsonian—Hewlett, that is, not Samuel.

CUBA

Doug Hostetter, writing in the January 1977 *Sojourners*, has come very close to the style of Anna Louise Strong, kind of a political travelogue. Touching down in Havana, he writes, "I almost felt like an explorer discovering a new land." He had been invited by the government to "gain knowledge of Cuba's government, society and people." The tour groups Malcolm Muggeridge witnessed were likewise invited by the government, with the expectation that they would return home and write glowing accounts for the folks at home. In this case, their expectations were justified.

Castro, a man who even managed to get himself denounced by Jean-Paul Sartre, is described as "serious about basic reform." Pierre Charette, who described Castro as "Robespierre," would certainly agree with that, though he might not call a Soviet-backed, one-party totalitarian dictatorship "basic reform."

Lois Krohler, an American missionary living in Cuba, exclaims to the tourists, "I was shocked to see the communist government accomplishing the very things I'd been praying for over ten years." What things? Nothing is mentioned, but, she says, "For the majority of the Cuban people, the revolution has meant an increase in the standard of living." Apparently at this point no one asked for proof of this or questioned why Cubans still sometimes depart their increased standard of living in rowboats and inner tubes. No questions. It was on to a tour of the Alamar housing project.

Here a priest in the delegation upset some people by mentioning that the Catholic church in New York City had been doing the kind of work for the poor that he saw happening at Alamar. Hostetter reports that the guide was "visibly irritated" with the comparison and promptly gave his testimony, which included all the things the revolution had given him—a home and a refrigerator—and his desire to go other places and fight for the revolution, for which he currently worked even on his days off. "I'll stay with communism," he said, his words ringing, "with the authenticity of the unrehearsed." Hostetter, a Mennonite and quite probably a pacifist, did not question the man's desire to take up arms so that others might have homes and refrigerators too.

The CDR, the Comité por la Defensa de la Revolución, is identified by Pierre Charette and virtually every Cuban refugee as the principle means of government control. The Cuban tour guides depict it as a kind of socialist Welcome Wagon, organizing classes on fire prevention, helping kids with homework, starting amateur theater groups and—more believable—discussing the latest speech from Fidel. Hostetter questions none of this. In fact at no time does he challenge any of the statements of his Cuban hosts. Can this be, as *Sojourners* promotional material says without a trace of embarrassment, "tough investigative journalism"?

The CDR is a block system of surveillance. Hostetter points to the fact that its officials are elected as an example of democracy at work in Cuba. But he further describes how democracy Cuban-style functions. With those who don't cooperate on voluntary work brigades, the CDRs "naturally respond with some hostility." Just what the hostility involves is not explained. If the hostility was nonviolent, Hostetter probably would have said so. Nor are we told why there should be any hostility at all if the brigades are, as claimed, voluntary.

Some Christians, the report continues, complained that they were not allowed to study in certain fields such as medicine, pedagogy, and psychology. Why? The guides explain that these individuals were not recommended by their community (for this read, "lacked the correct ideology and did not participate in voluntary brigades"). Again, not a peep from Hostetter.

This entire piece is highly recommended reading, a classic of the genre, with a level of sycophancy that truly defies belief. The article can scarcely be described as journalism let alone "tough investigative journalism." It contains not one word about forced labor camps, torture, scarcity of goods, shabby housing, the privileges of the new class, military conscription, and Soviet colonization. Should not the church speak out about such things?

Hostetter and people like him seem to accept Castro's claim that his revolution has not killed one citizen or tortured one prisoner. This claim is hollow. Poet Armando Valladares spent twenty-two years in Cuban jails, enduring horrible tortures. He was only released due to the intervention of French President Francois Mitterand. Humberto Noble Alexander, a Seventh Day Adventist minister, was arrested over twenty years ago for refusing to undergo ideological rehabilitation. He remained in jail after his term had expired, though Amnesty International and various church groups sought his release. Finally set free during Jesse

Jackson's visit to Cuba in 1984, he took issue with Jackson's praise of Castro, remarking that, "Castro is a Stalinist."[7] To radical Christians, this means "serious about basic reform."

A recent film about Cuba, *Improper Conduct*, directed by Nestor Almendros and Orlando Jimenez-Leal, won the Grand Prix at the twelfth annual Human Rights Film Festival in Strasbourg, France. Almendros interviewed exiles and refugees all the way from nightclub dancers to former government officials such as Martha Frayle and Carlos Franqui. All testify to the brutal repression of the regime. I met Almendros—himself a Cuban exile—at a Los Angeles screening of this movie and mentioned my own comparison of Stalin admirers with Castro admirers. "*Paralelo perfecto,*" he said.

Former fans of Cuba such as Susan Sontag have changed their minds completely. Pierre Charette preferred jail in Canada to living in Havana in a privileged capacity. Radical Christians like Doug Hostetter and *Sojourners* magazine may be the last devotees of this regime in the entire Western world. Should they decide to vacation in the "pearl of the Antilles," VIP treatment is guaranteed.

CHAPTER 15, NOTES
1. Danny Collum, "Anti-Communism: Our State Religion," *Sojourners*, November 1982, 19.
2. Danny Collum, "Critical Imbalance," *Sojourners*, October 1983, 6.
3. Jim Wallis, "Marginal Notes," *Sojourners*, December 1982, 27.
4. Jim Wallis, "A Matter of Idolatry, *Sojourners*, March 1984.
5. Jim Wallis, "Marginal Notes," *Sojourners*, October 1983, 13.
6. Robert Gillette, "US Clerics Assail Soviet Protesters," *Los Angeles Times*, 21 June 1984.
7. Don Shannon, "Freed Prisoners Split on Giving Jackson Credit," *Los Angeles Times*, 30 June 1984.

CHAPTER 16
NICARAGUA

The reign of God has arrived in Nicaragua.
Father Richard Preston,
Catholic Weekly

For more than a generation the Somoza family had ruled the Central American nation of Nicaragua as its own private fief, with the support, for the most part, of the United States. Anastasio Somoza, the last of the dynasty, was the quintessential Latin American dictator.

The situation in Nicaragua grew worse after the earthquake of 1972. Somoza seized every opportunity of extending his family's holdings. A personal friend who works for the Inter-America Tuna Commission in La Jolla, California, reports that Somoza owned every single tuna boat in the Nicaraguan fleet.

Somoza's encroachments in the early seventies turned even the Catholic church and the business community against him. The regime committed many serious violations of human rights and became universally unpopular. Many people, including myself, urged and supported his overthrow. The man had to go.

And go he did, due to a combination of factors. The Carter administration dropped some of their support and focused attention on Somoza brutality. Opposition groups formed a coalition with the revolutionary Sandinistas. The church backed them up. The Organization of American States demanded that Somoza resign and turn over the country to others. It was the first time they had made a statement of this nature. The assassination of newspaper editor Pedro Chamorro further unified the opposition. Somoza could only hole up in his bunker for so long. He was toppled in 1979, fled the country, and was eventually assassinated in Paraguay. And the Sandinistas ruled in his stead.

The Sandinista junta initially shared power with others on the State Council. This did not last, as democratically-oriented groups were edged out. Attempts by other groups to hold rallies were broken up. Non-Sandinista leaders of the anti-Somoza coalition, such as Violeta Chamorro and Alfonso Robelo, along with leaders of the business community, resigned in protest.

This trend continued. The Sandinistas, while claiming support for freedom, pluralism, independence, and so on, campaigned against independent trade unions, private businesses, democratic political parties, and the newspaper *La Prensa* (formerly anti-Somoza, now the last vestige of a free press in the country though heavily censored by the junta). In addition, they opened the country to Cuban and Eastern bloc military advisors and set up a block system of surveillance and informers based on the Cuban CDR model. Food ration cards are distributed on the basis of one's revolutionary behavior. Eden Pastora, a former Sandinista, saw the revolution betrayed and fled to Costa Rica to fight against his former comrades. Pastora was not alone.

Adolfo Calero, jailed by Somoza in 1968, heads a Honduras-based anti-Sandinista group. Indalecio Rodriguez, a life-long opponent of Somoza, also turned against the Sandinistas. His father had been a close friend of Nicaraguan patriot Augusto Cesar Sandino, from whom the Sandinistas take their name. Nicaraguan ambassadors have defected. The Sandinista regime has been militant and repressive.

The surest way to prevent any meaningful social change is to have a revolution, thereby freezing in place the repressive status quo the revolution creates. In fact, the essential distinction between the two regimes is that, under Somoza, human rights abuses represented the system in failure. Under the Sandinistas, the lack of human rights represents the system in triumph. Marxist rulers, once in power, must move quickly because people, when left to themselves (perverse beings that they are) undertake such bourgeois activities as buying, selling, fleeing the country, and generally doing what they want. This cannot be tolerated. Censorship must be implemented. Scientific socialism must be imposed. And if the people don't want it, well, that's too bad for them.

William Petersen of *Eternity* magazine interviewed Christian refugee families who had fled the country, claiming economic, religious, and political persecution. "Somoza," they explained, "never did anything for us, but at least he didn't bother us."[1]

What turned foreign admirers away from the Sandinistas more than anything else was the forced eviction of the Miskito Indians from the lands in eastern Nicaragua where they had lived for centuries. The Inter-American Commission on Human Rights, an arm of the Organization of American States, has compiled a 142-page report that says an undetermined number of Miskitos have been murdered, tortured, jailed, and relocated. Miskito villages and crops were burned, their livestock killed, and organizations that represented the Indians have been dissolved by the government. Fifty-one Miskitos were killed in the community of Leimus in December 1981, the report said. Thirty-five of these were killed on December 23 and buried in a single grave. Twelve more were killed the next day and thrown into the Coco River. The day after Christmas, the report added, an additional four were buried alive. Perhaps this was what Jesuit priest and junta member Ernesto Cardenal, a long-time admirer of Cuba, meant when he said:

> For us, the revolution is love. And by love we mean love
> of neighbor—making sure everyone has adequate nourish-
> ment, decent housing, medical services and education—in
> other words, a society of brothers and sisters.[2]

Compare the OAS report with an *Other Side* interview
with Pat Hynds, a Maryknoll lay missionary working in
Nicaragua. The interviewer asks: Do you see [the Miskitos]
relocation as a gross violation of human rights?

Answer: One could certainly argue that the relocation
of the Miskitos was a violation of human rights. The issue is
particularly difficult whenever indigenous people are moved
from their homeland. Yet, I'm convinced, after talking with
a number of people in the government and military as well as
the church, that the Sandinistas had no other choice.
Militarily, it was a move that had to be made.

Question: But, wasn't this move hard on them?

Answer: Of course, no one denies that it was a very difficult move physically—and that anybody who was healthy
had to walk. And it was a long walk. . . . When I would ask
the Miskitos, "Did you see anybody shot during your move?"
they would respond, "No."[3]

Elsewhere Hynds agrees that villages were indeed
burned to the ground (militarily, it was a move that had to be
made) and that people were "bitter and upset." She adds that
the Indians were moved to "protect their lives."

Now that it is manifest what the Sandinistas have
done, the radical Christians turn to apologies like this, from
Sojourners: "The young Sandinistas who now govern
Nicaragua have made some serious errors of judgement, have
sometimes hung on to their control too tightly, and have at
times been insensitive to racism and injustice."[4] Or, more
poetically, "Nicaragua is trying to be a light. Like any
candle, it sputters sometimes."[5] Others see things differently.

West German film director Werner Herzog (*Aguirre the
Wrath of God, The Mystery of Kasper Hauser,* and *Stroszek* are
three of his films) is no more a right-wing supporter of the

capitalist status quo than Jane Fonda. He recently showed up at the Cannes Film Festival after spending five weeks filming the Miskito Indians' guerrilla war against the Sandinistas. Though one of his films had won an award, he talked of little but Nicaragua.

> For some time I was intrigued by the Sandinista struggle. From Europe it looked particularly interesting, but I kept wondering why even some of the Sandinistas' closest friends deserted them. Now I've seen a small corner of the situation, and I understand.
> With good intentions the Sandinistas tried to bring 'scientific socialism' to the Miskitos. The story instead is one of deportation and concentration camps. A 10-year old told me how a 6-year old and a 2-year old were shot before his eyes. The atrocities are self-evident, and you don't have to be one side or another—and politically I'm not—to see what's going on.[6]

Herzog, whose film about the Miskitos will be released in 1985, predicts what the radical Christians see as the worst possible alternative. "Eventually," he says, "the Sandinistas will be overthrown." What he calls "atrocities," radical Christians refer to as "blunders," "problems," "errors," and, a favorite, "holding on to their control too tightly." So, I suppose, did Stalin hold on to his control too tightly. But then, the people unanimously kept voting him in, so he had no choice.

The timing of the religious left's championing of the Sandinistas also resembles the support of Sidney and Beatrice Webb for the Stalin regime. In the early days of the revolution, the Webbs maintained a certain aloofness. It was only when the planners began the forced collectivization that they dropped the question mark from the title of *Soviet Communism: A New Civilization.* It was at this time that the guided tours began.

Similarly, at the very time when the Sandinistas have declared themselves Marxist-Leninists, removed from influence many of the elements—business leaders, some churchmen, opposition parties—that helped them gain power, this is when American radical Christians begin their most earnest support. When indigenous people are murdered and driven from their homes (militarily, it was a move that had to be made), a military draft in force, the press censored, officials defecting, people fleeing, the church pressured to approve government actions, rationing and surveillance in effect, and the country full of Cuban advisers, this is the time Christian academics and journalists pick to make their tours and write their accounts. Some are cautious, taking a wait and see approach.[7] Others are highly laudatory.

Dr. Wayne Bragg of Wheaton College reports arriving with "grave misconceptions," such as the erroneous notion that the Sandinistas were repressive. "Instead," he writes, "we found a government of the people, by the people and for the people, including, for the first time, the very poor."[8]

It is not clear what Bragg means by a government by, for, and of the people. Were the Miskitos consulted about being removed from their lands? Did poor people vote for ration cards and a block system of surveillance? Did they request a military draft?

Bragg also follows the example of Hewlett Johnson, who referred to Stalin by his military title of Generalissimo. He dutifully calls the leader of the Sandinista junta Comandante Ortega.

Dr. Richard Pierard, history professor at Indiana State, informs his countrymen that they are "being part of the problem instead of part of the solution."[9] All they can offer, he says, is an "individualist" approach. In addition, they are susceptible to "the old anti-communist line." We are not told if this is the line that opposed Soviet genocide, the Nazi-Soviet pact, the invasion of Hungary, and so on. It is old, and anticommunist, and that ought to be enough, in his view, to make it undesirable.

Sojourners staff spoke of being able to wander about freely in Nicaragua, interviewing and photographing what they pleased. But their material includes no photographs of burned Miskito villages, no interviews with the editors of *La*

Prensa or opposition leaders removed from power, no mention of Archbishop Obando y Bravo, Humberto Belli, or Miguel Bolanos Hunter—dissidents all. It seems as if, for all those who return with glowing reports, there is full conviction that the Sandinistas are the true heirs of Saint Francis and that the United States (referred to in the new Nicaraguan anthem as "the enemy of mankind") is responsible for any and all evils in the area. There are no doubts in their minds that a speech by junta members Tomas Borge or Miguel D'Escoto (both priests) or Comandante Ortega cannot erase. But why go on?

Nicaragua is not yet fully totalitarian but certainly headed that way. Bayardo Arce, member of the Sandinista front, recently stated, "What a revolution needs is the power to enforce. This power to enforce is precisely what constitutes the defense of the dictatorship of the proletariat—the ability of the class to impose its will using the instruments at hand, without going into formal or bourgeois details. From that point of view, the elections are bothersome to us."[10] With the Soviet Union openly talking about deploying nuclear missiles there, this cannot be long delayed. As long as Nicaragua is barren of liberties, it will be barren of groceries as well.

The problems of the people—especially Christians—are serious indeed. I have endeavored to show only that the religious left's solution is not power-sharing, or negotiations with the former Sandinista opposition, or bringing to justice those responsible for the Miskito atrocities. No, their answer is to apologize for and thereby justify the repressive measures of the ruling elite. This will only make things much worse for the people that this elite are repressing.

Freda Utley pointed out that the Webb's whitewashing of Soviet purges and terror only encouraged Stalin to throw aside all restraint. The more radical Christians apologize for the Sandinistas and the more these apologies are accepted, the more the junta will implement draconian measures and the more individual Nicaraguans will suffer.

Christians sympathetic to the Nicaraguan or Cuban or Soviet juntas should not imagine that their efforts endear them to Marxists. Stalin openly called such morally fastidious people "rotten liberals," while at the same time accepting their services. As Djilas said, it is simply a matter of how useful anyone can be to the cause at any given time, as the Nazis were to Stalin.

A creative, ebullient people like the Nicaraguans, who produced the poet Ruben Dario and who have suffered for so long, deserve better. They now experience conditions at least as bad as those under Somoza but must put up with the added indignity of having these repressive measures excused by Christians abroad.

But the religious left sees the message of Christianity for people under Marxist regimes as one of full cooperation. "Is your lot hard, my son?" they say in effect. "Endure your privations with patience. Take your troubles to the Lord, but keep on working and obeying. As the Bible says, 'if anyone does not work, neither should he eat.' The comandantes are compassionate and wise and have things under control. Some day, when the yanqui enemy of mankind is defeated, things will be much, much better."

In this way, the Christian religion does truly become the opium of the people. What *Abbé* Custine said of Czar Nicholas I is true of Nicaragua: "It is only when the people submit blindly that a master can order tremendous sacrifices to produce very little."[11]

CHAPTER 16, NOTES
1. William J. Petersen, "Nicaragua, Nest of Conflict," *Eternity*, June 1984, 13, 33.
2. "At Issue: Nicaragua," *His*, January 1984, 18.
3. "Nicaragua: After the Revolution," *The Other Side*, September 1982, 38.
4. Joyce Hollyday, "A Plea from the Heart," *Sojourners*, March 1983, 54.
5. Joyce Hollyday, "Undoing Nicaragua," *Sojourners*, December 1982, 4.
6. John Vinocur, "Herzog Takes a Hard Swat at Treatment of Miskitos," N.Y. Times News Service, *San Diego Union*, 16 May 1984.
7. David Howard in "At Issue: Nicaragua," *His*, January 1984, 16.
8. "At Issue: Nicaragua," *His*, January 1984, 17.
9. "At Issue: Nicaragua," *His*, January 1984, 19.
10. Juan O. Tamayo, "Nicaraguan Decries Need for Vote," *Washington Post*, 8 August 1984, sec. A.
11. Abbé Custine, quoted in Freda Utley, *Lost Illusion* (Philadelphia: Fireside Press, 1948), 199.

SECTION 2
THE FUNDAMENTALS OF RADICAL CHRISTIANITY

CHAPTER 17
THE POOR

The poor, say those on the religious left, are the only ones who have the right to inscribe on their belt buckles, like German soldiers in 1914, the words *Gott mit uns*. Or as it is usually phrased: God is on the side of the poor.

People are poor for various reasons, not for one only, but one would never guess this from reading radical Christian publications. For instance, people can be poor because of their own lack of discipline and initiative. A steady provider can develop an alcohol or cocaine habit and plunge himself and his family into poverty. This group gets no sympathy from the Bible at all. In fact, they earn God's judgment.

Other poor people are genuine victims, suffering from injury, disease, or catastrophes such as famine and earthquake. The people of God are commanded to help such ones, because God himself is moved with compassion for them.

Still others are poor because of economic exploitation. Slavery is a historical example of this; South African apartheid and the East Indian caste system are contemporary versions. In case of exploitation, the victims have rightful claim to biblical justice.

A final group are the voluntary poor, who willingly give up affluent careers to better serve God and their fellow human beings. With ministerial salaries what they are, pastors could almost be included in this group en masse. Missionaries are another obvious example.[1]

The radical Christians see poverty as almost exclusively the result of economic victimization. Somehow, Western structural mechanisms like an open market and universal suffrage discriminate against the poor, while a controlled economy and one-party state such as that of Cuba is seen as somehow liberating and beneficial. It is assumed that the free enterprise model is the exploiter. Large corporations earn the radical's wrath in spite of the fact that, as Louis Fischer pointed out, Marxist governments are one huge corporation that controls *everything* and from which there is no escape, as there is from Nestle or Exxon. As Djilas shows, the capitalism that Marxists rave about no longer exists, but the radical Christians do not appear to have noticed. They are living in the past, nostalgic for the days of the dark satanic mills described by Charles Dickens and Karl Marx.

The exploitation model also begs the question of why living standards are higher in free economies. People *flee* closed societies like mainland China for better conditions in free enterprise countries. When refugees leave poor countries such as Mexico or El Salvador, they most often go to the United States, not to socialist Nicaragua. Why is this, if capitalist, open-market, politically free countries are examples of exploitive structures? If socialist dictatorships are so desirable why must they wall in their subjects? It bears repeating that even Hitler did not need such draconian measures.

The economic exploitation explanation for poverty demands a political solution. It assumes that those groups that have risen out of poverty have done so by political means. There is little if any evidence for this, as Thomas Sowell shows in *The Economics and Politics of Race*. The overseas Chinese, the Italians in Brazil, the Irish and blacks in America, and the Jews in many countries have generally kept their distance from politics. Where they have bettered themselves economically, Sowell shows, it has been the result of hard work, thrift, and personal sacrifice. These can yield results only in an open economic system. If there is a political solution, it lies in keeping the option for people to initiate their own economic activity.

The radical Christians explain poverty in the lesser developed countries by echoing the Leninist explanation first advanced to show why, contrary to what Marx predicted, capitalist workers got wealthier instead of poorer. Lenin said, in effect, that the capitalist bosses were exploiting poor countries and forestalling revolution at home by buying off their workers with high wages. Today this explanation is called the North-South Economic Dialogue. It fails to explain two things: why the lesser developed countries were poor in the first place, and why those that have had most contact with the allegedly imperialist powers have higher standards of living. This theory is popular because it advances an explanation of poverty based not on any inadequacies on the part of the lesser developed countries themselves, but only on moral deficiencies on the part of others. As Sowell writes:

> The enduring and fervent belief in imperialism as the cause of Third World poverty is difficult to understand in terms of empirical evidence. But this belief is much more readily understandable in terms of the high psychic and political cost of believing otherwise. These costs are high not only to some people in the Third World, but also to those in the West whose whole vision of the world depends upon seeing poverty as victimization and themselves as rescuers—both domestically and internationally. Many such people assume a stance of being partisans of the poor. But even to be an effective partisan of the poor, one must first be a partisan of the truth.[2]

One notices too a clear selectivity in the poor that the religious left chooses to champion. There are certain poor groups in their view worthy of love and support—and then there are others that are not. Jacques Ellul, whom radical Christians readily quote when he agrees with them, points out that groups like the Kurds, the Tibetans, and the monarchist Yemenites do not attract the attention of radical Christian groups. Why is this? Are they not as poor as American blacks or the Philippine underclasses? Why do radical Christians find them uninteresting? Ellul has a theory.

> Alas, the reason is simple. The interesting poor are those whose defense is in reality an attack against Europe, against capitalism, against the U.S.A. The uninteresting poor represent forces that are considered passé. Their struggle concerns only themselves. They are fighting not to destroy a capitalist or colonialist regime, but simply to survive as individuals, as a culture, a people. And that, of course, is not at all interesting, is it? But the choice violent Christians make has nothing to do with love of the poor. They choose to support this or that group or movement because it is socialist, anti-colonialist, anti-imperialist etc.[3]

To touch on the issue of labeling here, Ellul normally uses the term "revolutionary Christians" in his book on violence. Here, he substitutes "violent Christians."

Every issue of *Sojourners* and the *Other Side* bears out this interesting/uninteresting distinction. They support, for the most part, the aristocratic poor who have advocates in the UN and among film stars, such groups as the PLO and SWAPO. They say nothing about the others. Hence, their call to aid the poor lacks credibility.

Listening to the religious left, though, one wonders whether it is even desirable for any people to lift themselves out of poverty. The mindset of *Sojourners* and the *Other Side* reveals a tension between ameliorating conditions of the poor and exalting poverty as a virtue in itself. Theoretically, once people lift themselves out of poverty, they become part of the materialist mainstream and thus fodder for broadsides to "be more concerned about the poor."

On the one hand, they say poverty is abominable, and God's wrath is called down on us for allowing it (even though

Jesus Christ himself said the poor would always be with us). On the other hand, radical Christians lead us to believe that poverty is the only acceptable lifestyle for Christians and hence desirable. One cannot have it both ways.

The radical Christian ethic exalting poverty as a virtue in itself is a new version of the thirties intellectuals' deification of the proletariat. Arthur Koestler explained how eggheads like himself would willingly eschew their background and learning and lobotomize themselves just to be like Ivan Ivanov—the prototypical poor worker. Everyone unproletarian was dismissed as bourgeois. Being proletarian can even become a question of wearing the right clothing. Muggeridge described Orwell as decked out in "proletarian fancy-dress." The call to holy poverty is the same sort of social descent.

Can it really be contended that North American and European Christians are not concerned about the poor? American Christians give billions each year in charitable donations. Groups like the Salvation Army have been on the scene at foreign and domestic disasters before anyone else. They are the ones who run missions for derelict alcoholics—a case of the uninteresting poor if there ever was one—not Greenpeace or the Socialist Workers Party or the Sierra Club. What of the clinics, the counseling, the hospitals founded by religious groups? What of the acceptance of refugees from countries as diverse as El Salvador and Vietnam?

The March 1983 issue of the *Other Side* derided groups such as the Salvation Army for being "supportive of the political status quo," even though the Army also operates in Cuba and Nicaragua. In those countries, should they denounce the revolutionary status quo?

Government programs for the poor in the West have tended to be very generous. It has been said that the only budgets in the world larger than the American allocation for the Department of Health, Education and Welfare are the entire budget of the United States and the entire budget of the Soviet Union. In any case, it cannot be seriously maintained that Western governments do nothing about the poor. They even take in the poor created by their enemies, such as the United States' acceptance of the last flotilla from Cuba, many of whom were elderly and handicapped. Theoretically, the marvellous social services of the Cuban state should draw the poor from the four corners of the world.

When there have been earthquakes and natural catastrophes in various parts of the world, many Western nations have rushed material aid, medicine, and personnel to the scene. When Mount St. Helens devastates a huge portion of a state or when a tornado destroys 90 percent of a Wisconsin town, what Third World country constantly accusing the United States of being a grasping exploiter is there lending a hand? None. Western capitalistic nations, to their great credit, have continued to feed the hand that bites them. Some Third World leaders such as Julius Nyerere, whose country of Tanzania has received more aid than any other, have used transfers of funds to consolidate their own power, persecute their enemies, and continue economic experiments which have miserably failed.

I do not suggest that Western societies and their economic systems are perfect. But as the record shows, they tend to outperform their scientific socialist counterparts when it comes to providing for the poor.

None of us, especially those like myself who see a small role for government, should rest on our laurels. We need to be constantly exhorted to do more for the poor, within the church and without. God commands us to do so. Whether the religious left holds the moral qualifications to make this exhortation—along with their occasional appeal for donations for themselves—remains to be seen.

CHAPTER 17, NOTES
1. R. C. Sproul, "Biblical Economics: Equity or Equality," *Christianity Today*, 5 March 1982, 94.
2. Thomas Sowell, *The Economics and Politics of Race* (New York: Morrow, 1983), 229.
3. Jacques Ellul, *Violence* (New York: Seabury, 1969), 67.

CHAPTER 18
COMPASSION

When Jesus saw the multitudes, the gospels tell us, he was "moved with compassion."[1] The face of the Savior must have had a way of radiating his inner feelings. In another place we are told that Jesus, beholding the rich young ruler, "loved him."[2]

Compassion is a beautiful word but now so abased as to be barely usable. Politicians have been largely responsible for this. The late David Lewis of the Canadian New Democratic party (socialist) based his 1974 election platform on a call for a "Compassionate Canada," with the adjective in this case meaning, "More control by a government of its citizens' resources." The American Democratic party describes itself as, "the party of compassion." The word in this connection has come to mean something like, "the willingness of a representative to spend other people's money." Those unwilling to spend at acceptable levels are charged with "lacking compassion."

Jim Wallis outlined the radical Christian position on compassion in a September 1979 *Sojourners* editorial about Vietnamese refugees called "Compassion Not Politics for Refugees." Wallis concedes that the suffering of these people is "real," hardly an original revelation. He understates their perils, though, by neglecting to mention marauding Thai pirates who prey on the refugees and sink entire ships. He goes on to say that it is important to "get the facts straight" and that the coverage of the boat people has been "filled with inaccuracies, myths, misconceptions, and outright lies," though he neither mentions nor refutes any of these with facts of his own. The situation, we are told, "is complex and highly politicized and does not lend itself to easy explanations."

The shift away from simple explanations represents a change for the radical Christians. During the war it was very simple indeed; if you favored the American-South Vietnamese side you were wrong; if you favored an American pullout and the victory of the North you were right. It was simplicity itself. You were either part of the problem or part of the solution. But now easy explanations are eschewed, though Jim Wallis goes on to advance one himself.

Did the Vietnamese government, by any chance, have anything to do with this problem? Perhaps a bit. Their policies, wrote Wallis, were "harsh." One should pause a moment here and contemplate this adjective.

When the Reagan administration, a government elected by an overwhelming majority, put forth its 1980 budget, the cover of *Sojourners* thundered, ASSAULT ON THE POOR. Its writers readily use pejorative terms such as "militant," "oppressive," "reactionary," and "right-wing" for those who disagree with them. But when a revolutionary government strips people who merely want to leave of all their belongings, extorts outlandish "exit fees," then shoves them off to sea in rusty tubs that barely float, all this merits the description "harsh," something one might say of an overbearing high school principal. What word would they use if West Germany sent its Turkish minority packing on rafts in the North Sea? It would probably not be "harsh." But there is more.

After this scolding, Wallis says that the government "must take more responsibility for the orderly and safe exit of those who choose to leave." One looks for terms like "right" and "wrong" here, but the government simply must take "more responsibility," whatever that means. "In this respect," Wallis continues, "the revolution has become the regime and has begun to behave like governments everywhere." Really? Do governments everywhere do this kind of thing to potential emigrants? Does Iceland? Sweden? Belgium? Uruguay? As it happens, only socialist, revolutionary governments such as that of Vietnam have made crossing borders a tricky procedure, particularly on the way out.

It is not long before Wallis gets around to those who are, in his view, really responsible for the refugees—the United States, of course, even though this happened after the American forces left, something that Wallis urged for years.

Slipped into all this is an amazing sentence about the refugees themselves that should be read over several times, preferably aloud, and as slowly as possible. It says a great deal about radical Christian compassion.

> Many of today's refugees were inoculated with a taste for a Western lifestyle during the war and are fleeing to support their consumer habit in other lands.

Notice the sweeping generality ("many") applied to those who were inoculated with this criminal taste for Western lifestyle. And what does Western lifestyle mean? A tendency toward democracy? Mickey Mouse T-shirts? Freedom of religion? A large welfare budget? Abundance of the necessities of life? What? The imagery is that of the addict, fleeing to support his habit. The conclusion is inescapable: many of the refugees to some degree *deserve* what they are getting. Their crime was to be "inoculated with Western lifestyle." This, we are led to believe, merits banishment in leaking boats.

Imagine this scenario: You are a Vietnamese refugee, drifting on a derelict freighter in the South China Sea. Water is low; food almost nonexistent. You have no medical supplies or resources of any sort. Speedboats appear, full of heavily armed Thai pirates who rape the younger women, take some prisoner, steal everything they can find, murder some people outright, then sink the ship. You are left treading water, the cries of the drowning ringing in your ears. Wouldn't it be comforting to know that in secure, faraway America, the editor of a radical magazine, in an editorial about compassion, is announcing to the world that you are a Western junkie, fleeing to support your consumer habit in other lands?

The November 1979 *National Geographic* reports that Hong Kong officials picked up a pregnant woman and her child who were in two inner tubes being pushed through shark-invested waters by the woman's swimming husband. The consumer addiction of this group was indeed serious. Doubtless, they were after that color television set denied them under socialism.

Wallis denounces then-Vice President Walter Mondale for calling the Vietnamese government callous and arrogant and ends his editorial with, "Our response to the refugees must be one of active concern for the refugees, not out of political self-interest, but out of the compassion of Christ." All in all, quite a performance.

As it stands, this statement on the boat people is a piece of poltroonery ranking with the most bigoted and vicious I have ever read. It is similar to Anna Louise Strong dismissing the murder of kulaks on the grounds that Russia could get along without them, and explaining that Uncle Joe Stalin, after all, had only authorized what the people were already doing. The kulaks too, I suppose, in refusing collectivization, had thus inoculated themselves with Western lifestyle. Then too it has the ring of *Pravda* statements about "rootless cosmopolitans" who have the nerve to leave the Soviet Union.

One wonders what, by these standards, constitutes an attack if this editorial, as claimed, expresses compassion. *Sojourners* does give us some clues. In February 1980, Danny

Collum reviewed Bob Dylan's *Slow Train Coming* album. On one of the cuts, "Gonna Change My Way of Thinking," Dylan says he is going to "stop being influenced by fools." This was too much for Collum, who called it "accusatory" and "downright mean." One would almost think that Dylan was in the process of fleeing to support a consumer habit. Has the government of Vietnam ever been "downright mean"? Or just "harsh"?

Other questions arise. What of the Central American refugees pouring into the United States? Are they, too, fleeing to support a consumer habit? Should they stay at home and be happy in poverty? It hardly need be said what the implication is for those of us who live in the West.

Compassion? When a radical Christian says this, he really means compulsion. This attack on helpless refugees betrays a tunnel vision that is almost clinical. There is an ideological fungus on the political retina of radical Christians, blinding them to the faults of the dour Stalinists who currently run Vietnam. Before they would make any negative statements about a revolutionary (good) government, they attack the moral integrity of the victims of that government. It is assumed that the Vietnamese who remain are bound to do what they are told, even forced labor, euphemistically described in other *Sojourners* articles as "participating in the building of a new society." In the meantime, for the radical Christians, it is up onto Rosinante and off at a gallop to the next crusade on behalf of the downtrodden and oppressed through whose plight the United States can be denounced.

Michael Novak was once something of a radical Christian. As an antiwar activist, he even wrote speeches for George McGovern. When asked in an interview why he had changed his stance, he answered:

> One thing that encouraged me in that direction, in fact necessitated this direction, was the destructiveness of radical politics in foreign affairs. The terrible plight of the Cambodian people, the boat people of South Vietnam, and the

extraordinary suffering of the people of Vietnam today, have led me to realize that those of us who called for the end of the war in Vietnam unwittingly did something terrible. We caused even more destruction and more suffering, and we are guilty of the consequences of our actions. The least we can do is to learn from such things.[3]

Here is a man who, facing the facts, says that he was *wrong* about Vietnam. No such admission has been forthcoming from the radical Christians. This is a bit surprising.

At other junctures in recent history, *Sojourners* has been strong on apologizing. In the wake of the Iranian hostage crisis, Wallis wrote an editorial entitled "We Could Just Ask Them to Forgive Us,"[4] even though it was the Iranians, not the Americans, who took the hostages. The piece ends, "If our national pride and arrogance prevail over our reason and compassion, we will indeed reap the whirlwind." To apologize for someone else's wrongdoing, then, is to show compassion.

Perhaps the boat people deserve an apology for the things *Sojourners* has said about them; but, for now at least, being a radical Christian means never having to say you're sorry.

CHAPTER 18, NOTES
1. Matthew 14:14.
2. Mark 10:21.
3. "Interview with Michael Novak," *The Wittenburg Door*, November 1982, 24.
4. Jim Wallis, "We Could Just Ask Them to Forgive Us," *Sojourners*, January 1980, 3.

CHAPTER 19
PROGRESS

Barely anything that appears in publications of the religious left challenges the assumption that change is progress. In their view, the worse possible action anyone can take, particularly a Christian, is to defend the status quo in any way. The changes that are urged are of a structural, institutional variety and will, we are told, lead to social justice.

What this progressive view lacks is an historical perspective. A status quo composed of a divine-right monarch, an arrogant aristocracy, an authoritarian church, and an all-powerful police force is one thing. A status quo of a government of freely elected officials, a free press, universal suffrage, an open market economy, generous welfare programs, public education, and a police force that must read one his rights before arrest is something else. Yet the superstition of radical Christians is that to challenge the sort of institutions that exist not only in the USA but also in Canada, Lichtenstein, Belgium, and Holland is progressive; to hold that they are adequate is reactionary.

The test for anything is not whether it is progressive but whether it is right. A preponderant government that simultaneously dominated and took care of everyone was what feudalism was all about. Free enterprise democracy constitutes an improvement on that model. To identify progress with an ever-increasing government that serves as a kind of omnipresent wet nurse is to endorse a return to a modern form of feudalism. André Gide used these very words of the Soviet Union. In this system, the arrogant landowner is replaced by the arrogant bureaucrat.

Christian radicals, like mainline liberals, are slow to recognize that good intentions are not enough and that government programs set up to eliminate poverty sometimes only create dependency. Their main beneficiaries are often administrating bureaucrats. Yet it is the politician who most *talks* about poverty and social justice, that attracts the support of the religious left. Curiously, many politicians of this description—Teddy Kennedy and Pierre Trudeau for instance—are independently wealthy as a result of business acumen.

But a political candidate who is for free enterprise and business does not merit the support of the religious left because his *intention* is to help people make profits, regardless of what other benefits accrue to the community as a result of the increased economic activity.

In free societies, people have certain rights: life, liberty, and property, for instance. It is the role of government to guard these rights. The religious left confuses rights and goals. Living independent of government dole, in adequate circumstances, with enough surplus to help others, is an admirable goal. But no one can demand it as a right. It is the result of hard work—even, in many cases, of making a profit.

Of course, making a simple case for basic economic realities is less rhetorically appealing than denouncing the powers that be in the name of God. The truth is not always spectacular.

When it gets down to models of the kind of progressive societies radicals would have us emulate, the term "democratic socialism" emerges and Sweden, invariably, is named.

Yet Sweden is really a confiscatory, welfare-capitalist state. Democratic socialism as applied to, say, East Germany

(German Democratic Republic) really means undemocratic socialism. It is hard to believe that people would voluntarily assent to the continued total control of their lifes—especially control that resulted in reduced living standards. Democratic socialism—"socialism with a human face"—remains an illusion.

All governments have limits. No system can avoid the foibles of life. In Sweden, Denmark, and Holland, people smell bad, die young, go insane, have car accidents, contract terminal diseases, love each other, murder each other, and commit suicide much like the citizens of Brazil or Nepal.

There are no utopias. The advocacy of increased government control, far from being progressive, leads, as F. A. Hayek wrote, down the road to serfdom. One wonders why radical Christians lean so hard on political solutions.

CHAPTER 20
PACIFISM AND PEACE

PACIFISM

Malcolm Muggeridge noticed that Soviet military parades held particular fascination for Quakers and pacifists, whose hearts beat faster when the tanks rattled by and the planes droned overhead. In his essay, "Why I Am Not a Pacifist,"[1] he dealt with the mindset that does not allow international war but sanctions class war. When it was a case of international war, the pacifists pleaded their conscience; when it was class war, they sharpened their knives. This sort of stance, Muggeridge concluded, was not to be taken seriously.

Not much has changed since the thirties. For the most part today's radical Christians are advocates of precisely this kind of pacifism. Violence against capitalism, by these standards, is justified because it is for an allegedly good cause. Violence against socialism, on the other hand, is reactionary and evil and to be defended against by any and all means, with no moral qualms of any sort. The Sermon on the Mount and other texts are applied to anyone who believes that he may, as a Christian, serve in his country's armed forces. Such ones are urged not to fight. Special exceptions are made for class warfare.

John Alexander, in the February 1984 *Other Side*, admits that his "heart is not always in nonviolence." He speculates that he might have joined Dietrich Bonhoeffer in the plot to assassinate Hitler, qualifying this with the admission, "if I'd had the guts."

Bonhoeffer, apparently, had the guts. So did many others who found Hitler's National Socialist Reich so objectionable that some (including my own father) even chose to falsify their age to join the Allied forces. They apparently believed, as the New Testament states, that to lay down one's life for one's friends is an act of love.[2] It is nice to know that some radical Christians do not think that such people were all wrong. After all, had they and thousands like them been pacifists, there would now be no *Other Side* or even a radical Christian movement. Hitler's *Übermenschen* did not take kindly to conscientious objectors. Had Gandhi—so idolized by the religious left—tried his nonviolent tactics with the Nazis or Bolsheviks instead of a particularly squeamish British colonial satrap, he would have been arrested and never heard from again.

It is also comforting to think that if, say, South Africa invaded Denmark and began torturing welfare mothers, at least one radical Christian might urge a military response similar to the one even George McGovern advocated when Cambodians were being killed by the millions by Pol Pot. But the religious left reserves their greatest support for class warriors.

John Alexander expresses "deep sympathy" with Ernesto Cardenal for joining the armed struggle against Somoza. The Nicaraguan military—far and away the largest in Central America—carries special weight with radical Christians. How else does one account for Pat Hynds's explanation that the forced relocation of the Miskito Indians was "militarily . . . a move that had to be made"?[3] There is no sense of ethical struggle here; the Nicaraguan military said it, she believed it, and that was the end of it. Other examples abound.

For the most part, the religious left accepts the Marxist line that the only hope of social change in the Third World is militant revolution, sometimes soft-pedalled as social revolution. This is in spite of the fact that regimes as bad as that of Franco have been known to give way to an elected government without violence. If we must have a tyrant, as C. S. Lewis said, it is better to have a robber baron.[4] Robber barons all must eventually die, but a Marxist dictatorship of the proletariat is forever, immortal. Regimes of traditional despots have evolved into more liberal modes, even democracy, but no Marxist dictatorship has ever done so. In spite of this, radical Christians support revolution even though they don't do the heavy work. As in the cases of poverty and compassion, their call to pacifism—usually phrased in the Newspeak version of "nonviolence"—lacks credibility because of the double standard with which it is applied.

PEACE

Pacifists like to think their policies promote peace—and even refer to their ecclesiastical organizations as "peace churches." This overly generous designation implies that others are not as concerned with peace as they are. (Imagine a group calling itself "the righteousness churches.") It also begs the question whether the sort of policies advocated by pacifists do indeed make for peace. Do they?

This is very much an open question. There are no historical examples of conflicts being averted by one side disarming and declaring itself pacifist. While there is precedent for arms reduction, there is no historical precedent for disarmament.

What has happened, historically, is that weakness on one side has invited aggression, not deterred it. Hitler (who, like the Soviets, sponsored his share of peace conferences) was like a hotel thief walking down a hall, testing the doors, and, finding one open, barging in. He never attempted this with the Swiss but did request passage of his forces through their country, adding threats if this permission were not granted. "Nobody comes through here," the Swiss defense minister told him. And Hitler backed off, because Switzerland does not merely have an army, it *is* an army. But to credit military preparedness with deterring conflict is to be charged by radical Christians with militarism and idolatry. To trust the good intentions of someone such as Konstantin Chernenko incurs no such charges, even though the Soviet regime is merely a Slav version of Hitler's national socialism.

There has not been a war between the superpowers. This is what even Jim Wallis might call a fact. NATO has kept the peace and has not lost one man, woman, or child nor one square inch of territory in over thirty-five years.

This has happened because the Soviet Union, whose ideal Final Solution stipulates that the enemies of socialism will be vanquished, has been deterred from attack by a countervailing power in the West. Where there is no obstacle, as in Afghanistan, Hungary, and Czechoslovakia, they invade without hesitation.

The West once had the monopoly on nuclear weapons. No nuclear war occurred. Had the Allied powers so chosen, they could have gone on a rampage of conquest that would have made Alexander the Great seem like a rank apprentice. They did not do so. We do not know what would happen if the Soviet Union held a similar power. We do know that they, being good theocrats, believe that history has declared that they will prevail, and those who disbelieve this will be "swept away." They argue as cancer might if it could talk, saying that it must be right because it can kill us. To say that the dictatorship of the proletariat no longer believes this when its every act and word confirm it is, to me, beyond credibility.

A nuclear freeze, we are told by radicals, will bring peace. Such a freeze would have to be verifiable, and to verify anything in the Soviet Union it would be necessary to fundamentally alter their entire society. A verifiable freeze is a pipe dream.

Why the nuclear freeze movement did not leap into action before the USSR targeted hundreds of SS-20 missiles on European capitals is a mystery. Radical Christians gain martyr status by being arrested in protests in the West. If they truly believe that the USSR bears even equal responsibility for the current state of affairs, they should go and protest there. But the religious left has, in general, taken the easy route. The result is that they have made things more difficult, not easier, for elected leaders in the West. They turn their moral thumbscrews on those who are most vulnerable. And if anyone is not as worked up about the nuclear issue as they are, they are considered "sick," afflicted with "the wasting disease of normalcy."[5] In the nuclear freeze movement, radical Christians can employ apocalyptic, doom-gloom, almost hell-fire rhetoric with complete social safety, even approbation.

In addition to claiming a monopoly on peace, some on the religious left now purport to know the future. Ron Sider is more convinced than ever that a nuclear war is inevitable. How does he know? Scientists and "people in Washington" say so.[6] His *Nuclear Holocaust and Christian Hope*, co-authored with Richard Taylor, is kind of a religious version of Jonathan Schell's *Fate of the Earth*. Like Schell, Sider and Taylor rely heavily on shock tactics—describing blasts, destructions, bombs, blood, vomit, burns, screams. The front, fictionalized section of the book where this occurs is a combination snuff film and nuclear pornographic novel.

Merchandising comes later, the radical Christian version of Jesus watches and frisbees. Sider and Taylor advocate measures like displaying peace bumper stickers (surely a distinctively Christian approach), keeping photos of Hiroshima and Nagasaki on the coffee table instead of Ansel Adams, buying stationery with a peace motif, and subscribing to the right magazines including the "rigorously biblical" *Sojourners* for whose peace ministry co-author Taylor is a consultant.

To his great credit, Sider at least has the courage to carry his pacifism to its logical conclusion. The book may very well be the world's longest suicide note, suicide being the sure outcome of his nonmilitary defense plan, a new *Anschluss* on a larger scale.

The assumption is that, once conquered, we can all eventually settle down to a peaceful, neo-Scandinavian existence. Germany was once thoroughly conquered; they did not so settle down. Sider's arguments for *complete*, not just nuclear, pacifism are buttressed with proof texts, but remain to me unconvincing.

It appears they are unconvincing to the authors as well. After three hundred gruelling pages filled with countless usages of "must," "should," and "ought," Sider and Taylor make this astonishing statement: "The authors of this book do not claim to have all the answers."[7] Given this it is difficult to see their book as anything more than a public act of spiritual and political masturbation.

The best strategy for continued peace would seem to be the one that has kept the peace for nearly forty years: credible deterrence coupled with ongoing negotiations. But an immediate, verifiable freeze on nuclear pornography and hysteria certainly couldn't hurt.

The issue of peace should be linked with *freedom*. One searches radical Christian writings in vain for a passionate defense of freedom; after all, freedom is what enables Ron Sider to write, *Sojourners* to publish, protesters to protest, editorialists to editorialize, activists to be active, and pacifists to be passive.

On this question, the religious left is reactionary. Ronald Reagan, Margaret Thatcher, William F. Buckley, and Jerry Falwell talk much about freedom, hence radical Christians do not breathe the word. To do so would be to risk association with disreputable "right wing" types. On the whole, there is little deviation from the partisan left idea that freedom is nothing more than a bourgeois sham that any self-respecting soul would readily trade for a canard like "full employment" or at least a government job.

A personal note: Freedom is what enables me to live

and to write and to worship. It is my nonnegotiable. I will not trade it for some bogus peace on someone else's terms. Not only will I not surrender it lightly, I will not surrender it at all.

Any writer or Christian who repudiates freedom, in effect, demands his own destruction. For my part, I will not destroy myself. Like C. S. Lewis, I cannot be expected to be enamored of social change that would get me thrown into a concentration camp.[8] Likewise I cannot pretend that military force does not play a large role in maintaining this freedom. Totalitarian dictators are not influenced by talk. An appeaser is someone who thinks the crocodile will eat him last when, in fact, liberal types are generally the aggressors' first meal.

If a totalitarian steamroller were to give a lurch in my direction, Ron Sider and his friends may practice their non-military defense. That is their privilege. Unlike them, I do not have an agenda for everybody, only for myself. I know what I will do.

I will not be part of any *Anschluss*. I will fight.[9] If radical Christians choose to label me a "better dead than red" sloganeer, as Sider and Taylor caricature Harold O. J. Brown,[10] so be it. I would rather die on my feet than live on my knees. Nobody can make this choice for me. It is what I will do.

But wait just a minute. Perhaps those of us who feel this way are wrong. Perhaps we should bring our biblical faith more to bear on this subject. I am willing to listen to presentations of a better way, but not from people who, using the liberties purchased and defended by the lives of others, urge that free people surrender and disarm while defending the Sandinistas' incineration of Indian villages with the reasoning: "Militarily, it was a move that had to be made."

Everyone has his limits.

A final thought on the questions of peace and pacifism. The Christian pacifists who insist that some worthwhile purpose would be achieved by unilateral disarmament and capitulation to Soviet arms probably see themselves as fulfilling a martyr role in the ensuing *Anschluss*. But would this be the case? Michael Novak suggests a different and much more believable scenario:

> One notes with breathless admiration the self-image of such pacifists, concerning their personal virtue, spiritual heroism, and willingness to endure the Gulag. They imagine themselves to be Solzhenitsyns, Sakharovs, Orlovs. But they forget one thing. Their conquerors will not overlook the fact that such brave persons failed to lift a finger to help the five million persons now in the Gulag Archipelago; that such persons bowed docily to "the tide of history," and that such persons abandoned their Christian obligation to come to the defense of innocent peoples already suffering from unjust aggression. Faced with the naked power of the executioner, what further principles will they now betray? Will they not assist the authorities in urging the captive population to remain non-violent? Will they not repeat, with the executioners, that the citizens of the United States, perpetrators of "the Auschwitz of Puget Sound," *deserve* the most severe retribution? Will they not help convict their fellow citizens who urged earlier armed resistance of "crimes against humanity"? Will they themselves, in purest consistency, now testify against the generals, soldiers, journalists, theologians and others who supported deterrence earlier, in show trials designed to prove no more than what such pacifists have already alleged? Will they deny their own words?[11]

It will be interesting to see how radical Christian spokesmen such as Ron Sider answer these questions, if they have considered them at all.

CHAPTER 20, NOTES
1. Malcolm Muggeridge, *Things Past*, ed. Ian Hunter (New York: Morrow, 1978),48.
2. John 15:13
3. "Nicaragua: After the Revolution," *The Other Side*, September 1982,38.
4. C.S. Lewis, *Of Other Worlds* (New York: Harcourt Brace Jovanovich, 1967), 81.
5. Ron Sider and Taylor, *Nuclear Holocaust and Christian Hope* (Downers Grove, Ill.: InterVarsity Press, 1982), 291.
6. "Interview with Ron Sider," *The Wittenburg Door*, September 1979, 16.
7. Sider and Taylor, *Nuclear Holocaust*, 293.
8. Lewis, *Of Other Worlds*, 80.
9. Nehemiah 4:14.
10. Sider and Taylor, *Nuclear Holocaust*, 68.
11. Michael Novak, "Why the Church Is Not Pacifist," *Catholicism in Crisis*, June 1984, 35-36.

CHAPTER 21
STYLE

> When truth conquers with the help of 10,000 yelling men—
> even supposing that that which is victorious is truth; with
> the form and manner of the victory a far greater untruth is
> victorious.   Sören Kierkegaard

The leftist tradition has given us considerable literature and art, much of it of high quality. One thinks of poems by Pablo Neruda and novels by such writers as George Orwell, Dashiell Hammett, E. L. Doctorow, and Colombian Nobel Prize winner Gabriel Garcia Márquez, a close friend of Fidel Castro. The plays of Bertold Brecht have had staying power with theatrical audiences. In the field of cinema there is Lina Wertmuller, Luis Buñuel, and Costa Gavras. Even when their films are full of leftist catechism there is much in them that is purely aesthetic, used simply because it looks good or happens to be funny. One may call them consummate craftsmen, even artists. The religious left though—particularly the evangelical radical Christians—is not part of this tradition. With them it is utilitarianism all the way, a very bleak world indeed.

The first thing one notices about their writings is a complete lack of humor. I defy anyone to find five intentionally funny statements in all extant issues of *Sojourners* and the *Other Side*. The staff and writers take themselves very seriously, which should come as no surprise. If one interprets

Christ's kingdom as essentially of this world and one's primary role as a Christian to be changing the world through political power or even violence (social revolution), then one must view everything with great seriousness. The world is a tough place to change. People—even radical Christians—resist change.

One also notices that the images used in these publications are not chosen for elegance or beauty but for impact and manipulation. They are generally baleful or violent: mushroom clouds (very popular), guns, slums, soldiers, skull-like caricatures of people; photographs of emaciated children, outstretched hands, or people carrying protest signs; cover copy proclaiming slogans. In fact it could be argued that the description "magazine" is too generous and that the publications are more a monthly, thirty-page bumper sticker than anything else.

The church, particularly the Protestant church in the United States, seems to have an attraction to the visually banal, even the ugly. For example, too many church buildings look like warehouses for chain-saw parts. Ron Sider urges people to buy coffee-table photo books of Hiroshima and Nagasaki. The graphics of radical publications do not help cultivate the appreciation of art and beauty that the church so desperately needs.

Not only are radical Christian writings unappealing, but there is no *variety* in them. The same themes—peace, justice, social change—are endlessly recycled. Occasionally there will be an insightful film or book review on material of a different subject, such as the article on Annie Dillard's *Teaching a Stone to Talk* in the May 1983 *Sojourners*. There are some devotional articles, but these are rare. For the most part, the outlook is narrow. There is less here than meets the eye.

Compare this with, say, William F. Buckley's *National Review*, a publication no radical Christian worth his salt would hesitate in describing as right-wing. It is clearly political. There is much in it that is blatantly partisan; it reads at times like a Republican party in-house journal. But its interests are not narrow. There is much material on fiction, drama, religion, art, history, and a host of other topics, even cooking. Keith Mano writes a regular column that is probably the most unpredictable in the country, touching themes from book reviews to musings on hot tubs, with language full of arresting similes and words used just for their *sound*. John Simon, *National Review*'s film critic, highly recommended *Missing* and *Under Fire*, both of which feature the USA as villain. The critical apparatus is not political.

Compare too other religious magazines. *Eternity* and *Christianity Today* deal with issues of peace and justice, but not exclusively. And certainly not from one viewpoint. Every issue of the *Wittenburg Door* focuses on a different theme. A smaller publication, *Radix*, shares for the most part the purviews of radical Christians but also features some valuable material on art, poetry, and literature. Their interviews with critics such as Leland Ryken and writers such as Frederick Buechner and Larry Woiwode have been outstanding. The magazine is not boring.

Unfortunately, radical Christian publications are. It was not by accident that the *Wittenburg Door* used the title "Sobouring" in its satire, which included a classified ad offering lectures in "radical monotone," along with instructions on how to make everyone feel guilty and how to keep talking when everyone else has left the room.

Part of the reason for this is that, as Orwell pointed out, it is hard to write lucidly when defending blatant injustices. When, as André Gide said, the truth is spoken with loathing and falsehood with love, language becomes not an agent of clarification but of obfuscation. Radical journals do not say outright: "The Sandinistas were right to kill Miskito leaders, burn their villages, and move the population because by this strategy they consolidated their power." Rather, it would be stated something like this:

> It is a not unjustifiable assumption to say that the transfer of
> indigenous peoples to protected areas may have involved
> problems and blunders which, I think, some of those deeply
> committed to nonviolence among us might have second
> thoughts about. But in view of the lack of viable alternatives
> and the U.S. war of aggression, the move is probably best
> viewed as an unfortunate consequence of social change
> when the legitimate, long-range objectives are taken into
> account. The junta is trying to be a light, but sometimes the
> candle sputters.

Examples of this abound. The inflated, apologetic style
is itself a kind of euphemism.

Sometimes a writer will start with a soapbox hyperbole:
"This country has always assumed, either openly or just beneath the surface, that people are poor because they are
worthless and worthless because they are poor."[1]

It kind of holds you up for a minute. "This country has
always assumed"—does this mean everyone in the United
States? The Salvation Army? The Red Cross? Volunteers in
Service to America? The Mennonite Central Committee?
Who? If we knew who the author was talking about, we
could establish whether they have always assumed the poor
were worthless. Did the New Deal assume this? Do the millions allotted for Aid to Dependent Children? Unemployment insurance? Or were these cases where the deadly, universal assumption was "just beneath the surface"? The statement is demonstrably untrue. But the author is not engaging
in reasoned argument here but in political masturbation.

Commenting on radical style, *Wittenburg Door* editor
Mike Yaconelli noted two things. "To be honest, much of
the radical Christian style reminds me of the fundamen-
talists' style—their use of guilt, their call to conformity."[2] In
the pages of *Sojourners* we are often told that we *ought* to feel
guilty, even when the Soviet Union downs an unarmed pas-
senger airplane. Jim Wallis, who often enjoins such guilt, is a
Protestant. Flannery O'Connor observed that a difference
between Protestants and Catholics was that over-zealous

Catholics often disappeared into a monastic order and were never heard from again, whereas Protestants were free to run around wreaking havoc.[3] Similarly, in an earlier age, guilt-ridden radical Christians might have vanished into a monastery and flagellated themselves until the end of their days. Now, they have ad agencies and printing presses at their disposal and try to make the rest of us into flagellants too.

Ron Sider knows where the guilt button is. In *Nuclear Holocaust and Christian Hope,* he ponders the many good, decent people who want peace and justice but, at the same time, "are so afflicted with the *wasting disease of normalcy* that, even as they declare for peace, their hands reach out with an *instinctive spasm* in the direction of their loved ones, in the direction of their comforts, their home, their security, their income, their future, their plans" (emphasis mine).[4]

Isn't it a comfort to know that even if you display a normal "instinctive spasm" for your loved ones, if you are not as concerned about justice and peace as Ron Sider and Richard Taylor, why then you are *sick;* and not merely sick, you are afflicted with that wasting disease of normalcy. This is the man who recently claimed, "I have a passion for balance."[5]

All that remains is to be told that this charge of the disease of normalcy is made out of "compassion." The style is stern-as-death puritanism of the kind that makes people feel guilty just for being *alive* and quietly going about their affairs, as 1 Thessalonians 4:11 would instruct them. It borders on misanthropy. Susan Sontag, interviewed in the documentary *Improper Conduct,* remarked that such puritanism is "deeply embedded in the morals of the Left."

The rule seems to be: if it makes people feel bad, print it. Never mind that Jesus Christ put away a world's guilt, along with its sin, by his death on the cross. It is as if he had said, "I have come that they might have guilt, and have it abundantly."

Concerning Yaconelli's second point, he is absolutely right. The religious left's call to a radical commitment can most times be construed as nothing other than a call to be like them. Like Marine recruiters, they say, "Maybe you can be one of us." To this proposition, Yaconelli says, "God help us all."[6]

Though a lack of style is more at issue than anything else, there are other salient features such as exhibitionism and even hagiography. Radical writers are never reluctant to apply various versions of the word "deep" to themselves or their colleagues. They are "deeply committed" to nonviolence or "deeply involved" in social justice. Jimmy Carter and Walter Mondale likewise described themselves as "deeply religious." Remarks Congressman Paul Simon, a Lutheran, "When Carter says he is 'deeply religious' I am troubled by that. I don't know many people who are deeply religious who describe themselves that way."[7] I don't know many either.

Likewise, I don't know anyone attempting to live a simple life who tells me how much personal spending money he is allotted each month. The masthead of *Sojourners* used to announce that each member had "$15 a month spending money," about fifty cents a day. If this is not a flaunting of poverty then what is?

Radical Christian promotional material often claims "the Government is worried" about the activities of people such as themselves. This claim of access to the emotional life of politicians is surely inflated. Just how much sleep any government loses over religious socialists is uncertain. But it is possible to guess.

Neither do radical Christians hesitate to publicize how much they pray and on what subjects. Jim Wallis reveals the entire content of a prayer meeting held after the death of Leonid Brezhnev.[8] Among other things, they asked forgiveness for anticommunism. Maybe I am wrong, but I always thought that prayers were a private matter to be carried on in secret before God and not to be exposed in the pages of a magazine, ostensibly to give the rest of us an example of what we ought to be doing.

There is something pretentious about it all, an externalizing of piety, changing homilies into political programs and exhortation—or even prayers—into demagoguery. Accordingly, along with the self-advertising approach, a lot of name dropping goes on as well (Merton, Martin Luther King, Stringfellow, Gandhi, Daniel Berrigan) interspersed with radical jargon like "mammon," "oppression," "the powers," and so on. It is all here, a regurgitation of every platitude and shibboleth of recent memory.

In addition to name dropping, there are examples of gratuitous verbal abuse of a most puerile nature. Gil Dawes, a Methodist minister and a member of a group called Christians for Socialism (who obviously has no qualms about the socialist label), writes compassionately on the subject of labor disputes: "I am concerned with those *mealy-mouthed* preachers, priests and rabbis who say they don't take sides, that they minister to *all* sides" (first emphasis mine).[9] Anna Louise Strong, in a similar vein, strove to see only one side of a question. But even Hewlett Johnson never called opponents mealy-mouthed.

In some ways, the style of the religious left reminds one of the conspiratorialists of the John Birch Society. America, in their view, invented evil. When the Ayatollah Khomeini calls the USA "The Great Satan," radicals concede that the man does have a point. Behind every injustice in the world, it seems, is a capitalist-militarist-racist-CIA-multinational corporation plot. The Birch folks who see communists behind every rock are simplistic. So is the demonology of radical Christians. Many articles read like a translation of an angry United Nations speech by someone from the government of Albania.

The negative, querulous tone of radical writing leads one to wonder if anything would satisfy them. The reader is not to be blamed if he imagines a radical Christian journalist sent to Valhalla or Shangri-la returning with a chronicle of woe and an agenda for "serious reform."

The style, then, of radical Christians is a mixture of slogans and platitudes, political harangue, flagellation, puritan moralizing, fundamentalist conformity, and exhibitionism —all of it dished up in boring prose and dull format. If there is a drearier spiritual or aesthetic combination around, I haven't seen it, nor want to. Adapting a saying of Voltaire, one can't agree with everything radical Christians say, but one would die for the right not to hear it.

The View from Outside

Though the radicals themselves, according to all appearances, are as serious as it is possible for humans to be, others find them risible. Mike Yaconelli and the *Wittenburg Door* are not the first to see their enormous comic potential. George Orwell's *Keep the Aspidistra Flying* lampoons the armchair socialist, comfy in a capitalist society. The contradictions and buffooneries of the left-wing political journalist jostle in the pages of Malcolm Muggeridge's *Winter in Moscow* and *In a Valley of This Restless Mind*. Auberon Waugh's *Who Are the Violets Now?* is also worthy of attention. P. J. O'Rourke of *National Lampoon* treated readers of the November 1982 *Harpers* to a nonfiction comedy about a tour sponsored by the Society of Soviet American Friendship. The account is priceless. So is Woody Allen's film *Bananas*. Set in the imaginary country of San Marcos, it pokes fun at revolutionaries and their adherents.

French filmmaker Louis Malle recognizes that the humorous possiblities of those radicals who are also religious are indeed great. The absurdity of combining Marxism and Christianity, whose basic tenets are opposed to each other, is all too apparent, but he treats the subject with subtlety. In his film *My Dinner with Andre*, a film director reminisces about a Catholic priest on Long Island. He was, Andre says, "One of those priests who was always talking about communism and birth control." Doubtless, to make such a callous joke about a man who was obviously deeply committed to social justice and preventing overpopulation, Andre would have to be stricken with some wasting disease, like normalcy.

In the twentieth century, some of the biggest jokes are unintentional.

CHAPTER 21, NOTES
1. Danny Collum, "Crossing the Canyon," *Sojourners*, January 1980, 3.
2. Mike Yaconelli, "The Back Door," *The Wittenburg Door*, September 1979, 32.
3. Flannery O'Connor, *The Habit of Being*, ed. Sally Fitzgerald (New York: Farrar, Strauss & Giroux, 1979), 517.
4. Ron Sider and Richard Taylor, *Nuclear Holocaust and Christian Hope* (Downers Grove, Ill.: InterVarsity Press, 1982), 291.
5. Ron Sider, "Let's Get the Church Off the Soapbox," *Christianity Today*, 16 March 1984, 54.
6. Yaconelli, "Back Door," 32.
7. "Interview with Paul Simon," *The Wittenburg Door*, July 1980, 24.
8. Jim Wallis, "Marginal Notes," *Sojourners*, December 1982, 27.
9. Gil Dawes, "Let My People Go," *The Other Side*, June 1982, 21. Dawes further states that "right-wing fundamentalism" provides "the mythological support for fascism."

CONCLUSIONS

Some future Gibbon[1]—assuming there is one—will have a lot of fun looking back on the spectacle of a militant pacifism, a Marxist-Christian dialogue, and pious clergymen composing odes to Joseph Stalin's depth. One can join in the mirth today, but ultimately, as Arthur Koestler wrote, the situation is no laughing matter.

> The well-meaning "progressives of the Left" persist in following their old, outworn concepts. As if under the spell of a destructive compulsion, they must repeat every single error of the past, draw the same faulty conclusions a second time, re-live the same situations, perform the same suicidal gestures. One can only watch in horror and despair, for this time, there will be no pardon.[2]

Surveying the current religious left, one could think that they had set out to duplicate the earlier record. It is as if a torch had been passed, upside down. They continue to judge socialism by its promises and postdated checks, and not by its record. They are inquisitors with Western democrats and sycophants with Marxist revolutionaries. They have made Christianity the agent of protest and change in the West, but exhort those Christians under Marxist dictatorships to stay put, accept their shabby conditions happily, work hard and not complain. This brand of Christianity, like Marxism itself, is the new opium of the people; it makes change difficult if not impossible. In addition, radical

Christians have ignored the testimonies of Koestler, Muggeridge, and many others.

But why does it happen? Why are well-meaning religious people continually drawn to phantom kingdoms of heaven on earth, even to ones that persecute Christians? Why, when they are often such smart and caring people, do they employ their faculties in defense of a system founded on coercion? Several answers have already been suggested by the authors covered in this book.

Revolution, like revivalist religion, puts down the high and mighty and exalts the humble and meek. Since the Bible does command care for the poor, there is a sharing of rhetoric. Revolutionaries say they are concerned for the poor. Radical Christians believe them. Unfortunately, it is often forgotten that once the poor and humble and meek are exalted, they too become the high and mighty, themselves fit to be put down.

Reaction has something to do with it. Some radical Christians were brought up in an extreme God 'n' country fundamentalism that views America as the Promised Land, Americans (viz. white, middle-class, nonsmoking but tobacco-farming Republicans) as the Chosen People, and just about everybody else as suspect. Brought up in such circumstances, radicals come to associate all opposition to Marxism with some hokey radio evangelist pleading for donations to help him fight godless communism. America is a great place but not the only place. It has no corner on God's favor. But, unfortunately, radicals often jump from this extreme to its opposite number. Or they repeat the line that the two superpowers "mirror" each other. Examining this idea at the height of the cold war, French philosopher Raymond Aron concluded that, far from mirroring each other, the American system was the "exact opposite" of the Soviet model.[3] But why should radicals be expected to notice such things?

Those who admire the dictatorship of the proletariat in its varied forms do so because they would like to be a dictatorship of the proletariat themselves. As Muggeridge wrote, they are frustrated revolutionaries. They share the revolutionary ideals of collectivism[4] and social engineering but have little stomach for what it takes to get the job done—terror—since they are also deeply committed to non-violence. Thus, their admiration is unbounded for those who, with no second thoughts or moral qualms, actually seize total power, repress and eliminate opposition, and shovel people around like concrete. It is a form of vicarious experience, like a mild-mannered clerk getting his kicks from televised football or wrestling.

The simplest but probably most accurate answer is that there is a death wish at work in the world and that this is part of it. How else can one explain Christians admiring a system that would make them unnecessary? There is nothing rational about it. Yet many in the West, not just radical Christians, tend to sympathize with developments that would mean the end of their societies, their religions, themselves, and the rest of us with them. They blow the trumpet that brings their own walls tumbling down. This is how civilizations end. Not with a bang or even a whimper, but with a death wish.

And people believe lies, not because they are plausible, but because they want to believe them. How else can one explain religious writers, clergy, activists, and college professors who are determined, come what may, to believe discarded dogmas, to overlook any brutality, to accept any explanation as long as it comes from the proper comandante. They want to preserve intact the hope that some of the most militant and obscurantist tyrannies ever to exist on earth can be relied upon to champion peace, Christian social action, the elimination of poverty, the brotherhood of man, and all the other good causes to which they have dedicated their lives. They believe this, not because of any evidence, but because they want to.

How best to describe them? This too has been done before. When Orwell was writing *Animal Farm*, he discussed the project with Muggeridge who suggested that, at the point where the pigs mastered walking on two legs, he should introduce a host of fellow travelers, led by the Dean of Canterbury, shuffling along on all fours. Orwell found the idea funny but turned it down. It fits the present situation perfectly.

Porcine acts such as Khrushchev's animal bellowing and stomping are no longer the rule. Rather, listening to Soviet spokesmen such as Georgi Arbatov, one would think they sat up late memorizing George McGovern tapes. Other emissaries of dictatorships have also mastered the subtleties of liberal-speak. At this very point in history, when the pigs walk and talk like humans, along comes a bunch of Christians walking on hands and knees. One would think that, in a reversal of the Gadarene story in the gospels, the spirits of the pigs had been cast out and entered into men and women. It is a parable for all time.

CONCLUSIONS, NOTES
1. English historian Edward Gibbon (1737-1794).
2. Arthur Koestler, *Arrow in the Blue* (New York: Macmillan, 1952), 235-36.
3. Raymond Aron, *The Century of Total War* (New York: Beacon Press, 1955), 357.
4. Christian socialists usually base their collectivism on Acts 2:44-46.

AFTERWORD

This has not been a moderate critique. A moderate, as Chesterton said, was someone who believed that a house should be moderately clean. Better to do the whole job. The Christian faith is being turned by some into a public relations apparat for totalitarianism, much as if some early bishops had gone to the coliseum and cheered for the lions. This calls for more than moderation.

Accordingly, I have not held back most things I wanted to say—especially about the radical evangelicals. But if the reader cares to survey other books of this sort, especially those by Muggeridge and Orwell and *The God That Failed*, it will be seen that I have not been excessive, certainly no more so than, say, *Sojourners* is itself. I offer no apology.

No one should interpret this critique of the religious left as absolving them of social responsibilities. The failure of radical solutions is all the more reason to fulfill biblical responsibilities to the poor and needy. Much is given, much is required.

No measures are here advocated against the religious left; no serpentine conspiracy theories advanced; no charges proferred that any individuals are apostates or traitors or foreign agents or anything of that sort. Behind the phenomenon of leftist Christians stand not nefarious plots and cabals, but two things: the tyranny of the General Idea (in this case, the socialism = Christianity equation) and a death wish.

Neither should radical Christians be shunned. We should read the radical publications, publish radical authors, invite radical speakers to our conferences and churches. We should listen to what they have to say. The author asks only that the same scrutiny be brought to bear on them that they so freely impose on the rest of us with individualist views.

In the interest of learning, I suggest one other measure. We are not to pretend that radical Christians are something new. To understand them better, we should study their spiritual and political ancestors.

Thus, whenever religious radicals hold forth, those in attendance should pause to remember the patriarchs. First, a moment of silence for Anna Louise Strong, the feisty, self-described motor-minded girl from the Midwest, with her doctorate on the psychology of prayer and her articles and fairy tales written for a fundamentalist magazine. Remember her determination to change the world. Recall her playing a game to see how much she could put over on the readers of the Hearst newspapers and such publications as *Harper's* and the *Atlantic*. Remember her deep commitment, her honorary Red Guard status. Bear in mind how, knowing the facts all along, she kept silence for the cause and was at long last rewarded with a state funeral by her mentor and Great Helmsman, Mao Tse-tung.

Likewise, a moment of silence for Rev. Hewlett Johnson, meeting with comandante Stalin and being duly impressed with his humility. Remember his declaration that under the aegis of this great leader, the kingdom of Christ was being bought to the world, even as the undesirable elements were being swept inexorably away. Call to mind his denunciations of the United States and compare them with the new version. Remember too how he won the Stalin Peace prize, and how this must have thrilled him. Finally, remember his greatest distinction of all: an entry for Hewlett Johnson in the *Great Soviet Encyclopedia* longer than the one for Jesus Christ.

As the apostle Paul might say, "meditate on these things." Like Mary, "treasure these things in your hearts." Compare them with what you hear when a radical Christian band identifies a new gulag as God's country. Remember the reports of apple-cheeked dairy maids and mountains of wheat, made during the world's first man-made famine. Like the inhabitants of *Animal Farm*, look from one group to the other and see if you can tell which is which.

Perhaps too one could pause in hope. Even the old testament of totalitarian apology did have an evangelistic side. Listening to people like Strong and Johnson convinced a young and searching Malcolm Muggeridge that no earthly solution could be found, no earthly battle won. He has since turned his attention to the City of God, which man did not build and which man cannot destroy. There may be others like him in the audience. The radical Christians may yet help bring them to God.

SELECT BIBLIOGRAPHY

I have not felt it necessary to duplicate the notes of source materials used in this book. All the works referred to are highly recommended reading on their respective subjects.

However, for those who wish to further study socialism and the support for it among intellectuals and clergy in the West, I list those books that I feel are most worthy of the serious reader's attention.

Arendt, Hannah. *Origins of Totalitarianism.* New York: Harcourt Brace Jovanovich, 1966.

Caute, David. *Fellow Travellers: A Postscript to the Enlightenment.* New York: Oxford University Press, 1973.

Conquest, Robert. *The Great Terror.* New York: Macmillan Publishing Co., 1968.

Crossman, Richard, ed. *The God That Failed.* New York: Harper, 1949.

Djilas, Milovan. *The New Class: An Analysis of the Communist System.* New York: Praeger Publishers, 1957.

Hayek, F. A. *The Road to Serfdom.* Chicago: University of Chicago Press, 1944.

Hollander, Paul. *Political Pilgrims: Travels of Western Intellectuals to the Soviet Union, China, and Cuba.* New York: Oxford University Press, 1981. The most exhaustive, scholarly work; includes a wealth of sources.

Johnson, Paul. *Modern Times: The World from the Twenties to the Eighties.* New York: Harper and Row, 1983.

Lévy, Bernard-Henri. *Barbarism with a Human Face.* New York: Harper and Row, 1979.

Muggeridge, Malcolm. *Chronicles of Wasted Time.* New York: William Morrow and Co., 1973.

Orwell, George. *Inside the Whale and Other Essays.* London: Penguin Books, 1957.

SUBJECT INDEX